The Genesis Code

Revealing the Ancient Path to Inner Freedom

Related books by Richard L. Haight

The Warrior's Meditation
Unshakable Awareness
The Unbound Soul

The Genesis Code

Revealing the Ancient Path to Inner Freedom

Richard L. Haight

Shinkaikan Body, Mind, Spirit LLC

www.richardlhaight.com

ISBN: 978-1-956889-00-0

Library of Congress Control Number: 2021920348

Disclaimer:

1. Some names and identifying details have been changed to protect the privacy of individuals.

2. This book is not intended as a substitute for the medical or psychological advice of physicians or psychologists. The reader should regularly consult a health practitioner in matters relating to his or her physical or mental/emotional health and particularly with respect to any symptoms that may require diagnosis or medical attention.

Published by Shinkaikan Body, Mind, Spirit LLC

www.richardlhaight.com

Contents

Introduction

In this book, as the title intimates, we will explore a secret teaching found in the ancient Book of Genesis. To get an accurate understanding, we must be careful not to assume that ancient people taught openly as we do now. Modern people reading ancient scripture might assume that the overt teachings portrayed in those texts reflect what the original authors actually taught and valued. That assumption is probably incorrect for a number of reasons. We are fortunate to get a rare glimpse of the disparity between the true teachings and what is shown publicly through the canonical accounts of Jesus.

Did you know that Jesus' true teachings were secret and that what we are taught in The Holy Bible may not include his core teaching? Quotes attributed to Jesus from the books of Matthew, Mark, and Luke state plainly that Jesus withheld his true teaching from everyone except his disciples. The statement is found in all

1

three of the synoptic gospels, giving it much more weight. As all three accounts make Jesus appear unempathetic to the masses, a portrayal that early Christians would likely not want advertised, the statement is likely true.

Matthew 13:10-13 quotes Jesus as follows:

> 10 The disciples came to him and asked, "Why do you speak to the people in parables?"11 He replied, "Because the knowledge of the secrets of the kingdom of heaven has been given to you, but not to them. 12 Whoever has will be given more, and they will have an abundance. Whoever does not have, even what they have will be taken from them. 13 This is why I speak to them in parables: "Though seeing, they do not see; though hearing, they do not hear or understand."

Mark 4:10-11 contains almost the exact same account:

> 10 When he was alone, the Twelve and the others around him asked him about the parables. 11 He told them, "The secret of the kingdom of God has been given to you. But to those on the outside everything is said in parables 12 so that, "'they may be ever seeing but never perceiving, and ever hearing but never understanding; otherwise they might turn and be forgiven!'"

Luke 8:9-10

> 9 His disciples asked him what this parable meant. 10 He said, "The knowledge of the secrets of the kingdom of God

has been given to you, but to others I speak in parables, so that, "'though seeing, they may not see; though hearing, they may not understand.'"

That Jesus kept the true teachings secret should not come as a surprise, for the Gospels clearly tell us that is the case. Many ancient tradition holders work hard to protect their knowledge. What they reveal to the public is often far from what they practice in secret.

I happen to be a tradition holder of several ancient samurai arts. You could train for years reaching the higher levels, thinking you know what the practice is about, only to discover that vital secrets that unlock the true power of the system remain hidden from outsiders and advanced students alike. Even among the highest-level students, most never access those secrets and continue to practice, unaware of the "gems" or knowledge secreted within the system.

One might wonder why people would hide their art or wisdom in this way. In the case of the arts I inherited, historically it was considered vital to hide the knowledge from your enemy, who could use that knowledge against your clan if they acquired it. Usually, the deepest secrets were only taught to a handful of people, typically close relatives of the master. Many ancient samurai arts have been lost or watered down due to this kind of secrecy.

Imagine passing your art on to only a few trusted individuals who then die or otherwise fail to pass it on. Absent fully trained successors, the remaining students take over and teach the system unaware that they are missing vital knowledge. The art carries on in name, lacking much of its true value.

The question is how one knows when one has truly uncovered and embodied those secrets. In the case of the systems that I received, you know because you can effortlessly do everything that the teacher can, and you can create new methods instantly. You are martially free, and as a result, the entire art is transformed—it's a startling difference.

Fortunately, the incredible abilities of the masters within the arts that I study are well documented, so it's easy to verify if you've embodied the inner teachings based on your abilities. When you achieve that level of embodiment, the teacher, at least in my lineage, explains why these things are kept secret, and you are awarded the license of full mastery.

Now consider the ancient Jews who are said to have been enslaved in Egypt for a century and persecuted relentlessly wherever they went thereafter. How carefully would they protect their inner secrets? Maybe what we know of Judaism is just the surface level teaching.

What if the most closely guarded secrets of Judaism and Christianity were lost thousands of years ago? How would we know it? We wouldn't, and neither would they. It seems I have found just that kind of secret in Genesis, the first book of The Holy Bible. I believe it may be the lost "truth that sets you free."

That is a bold statement, I know. With a statement like that, this book has a lot to live up to; after all, this was the promise of Jesus some 2000 years ago, when he said, "Know the truth and the truth will set you free."

Stated more precisely, it's not just the state of knowing the truth but the proper application of that knowledge that sets us free. And who would not want to be set free? The answer depends on the type of freedom we are referring to and the price of that liberation.

The freedom we are talking about here requires commitment and responsibility to realize and maintain. A lot of people don't want to make the necessary commitment or take on the required responsibilities, and that is very understandable. After all, modern life is so rushed and busy. Why would we want to take on a new challenge in light of just how time-constrained we already are?

Because time is something we can never get back, let us first make sure this book is aligned with your goals. Please consider several questions as you read the next few paragraphs:

- What kind of "freedom" is the book referring to?
- Do you desire that type of liberation?
- Are you willing to take on the challenge of realizing your true nature?

First, let's explore the meaning of liberation as I use it here. I do not mean freedom from physical death, sickness, pain, misfortune, or ill treatment; as history shows, without exception, those experiences happen to everyone. Rather, I refer to freedom of a psychological and spiritual nature.

By "freedom," I mean freedom from compulsive self-absorption. Freedom from arrogance, resentment, and condemnation. Freedom from the seemingly endless cycles of blame, shame, and guilt. Freedom from unhelpful thoughts and beliefs and the torments of anxiety and emotional depression—regret of the past and fear of the future. Ultimately, I mean freedom from that which misleads our minds and emotions.

The truth hidden in the book of Genesis is really a guiding principle that lies at the very root of human perception. As you start to realize and correct your life based on this principle, it's normal to experience some degree of inner resistance, as if something within you feels threatened.

You may have moments of visceral fear for no apparent reason. Give it a little time, and you will see that it passes. You may notice little or no fear at all until quite late in the process. That's fine. That said, almost everyone will experience some degree of psychological resistance to the process, as aspects of our identity that no longer serve but that still feel like us start to fall away.

With regard to resistance, the best way forward is to accept it as a natural part of the process without trying to escape or avoid it. The resistance that you might experience is subconscious, almost instinctive, and therefore, not your fault, so there is no real reason to be too concerned about it.

To successfully apply *the principle* requires letting go of inner baggage. We could look at *the principle* metaphorically as an altar fire that burns away the falsehood within us, leaving only that which cannot burn—the true you.

Through the burning process, you will likely experience moments of catharsis. And with those releases, that which cannot burn inspires, guides, and clarifies your life. Through the burning process, your life becomes vibrantly balanced and open in ways you might find hard to imagine while reading this passage. Practically speaking, you're ever freer of the mental and emotional chaff that has been holding you back from your most authentic life.

The principle at the heart of this text is neither ideological, philosophical, nor religious in nature; nor is it a "positive thinking" scheme. Instead, what emerges from this process is more fundamental to the nature of being than such mind-conjured strategies. In fact, *the principle* works to undo unhelpful mental strategies, many of which fall into the categories of ideology, philosophy, and belief.

Successfully applying this freshly rediscovered truth to your life does not mean life will be easy. No matter what you do, life is going to be challenging. The question is whether you wish to face the challenges with your eyes and heart fully open. If you want that ability, that sort of freedom, then *The Genesis Code* is likely for you.

Know that *the principle* does not require a religious belief, which means it works even if you do not believe in God. *The principle* does not discriminate against culture, ethnicity, skin color, class, nor status in the world. It works exactly as you apply it—no more, no less.

The principle resides at the level of perceptual unity, where we are all the same. To get to that level of unity requires us to soften beliefs that prevent us from fully accessing that level of perception. Are you willing to question and soften your beliefs, especially the comfortable ones? It won't work if you refuse to surrender at least that much.

If fully employed, the hidden truth of Genesis will revolutionize the way you see yourself and life by dissolving inner divisions and unhelpful motivations that cause all manner of disharmony. The result of such dissolution is an embodied sense of oneness with life, clarity, and lightness of heart. How much unity, clarity, or lightness you feel will depend on how deeply you open and how thoroughly you apply *the principle* in your daily life.

I'm not a reverend, pastor, monk, or priest. I have never been to seminary school, and I have no intention of doing so. In fact, I haven't attended a religious gathering of any sort in more than 25 years. As I stated already, I'm not a follower of religion. Instead, I am a lifelong practitioner of mind-body awareness arts—martial, meditative, and therapeutic.

That brings us to the question of how I discovered the code. Since childhood, I have been a regular recipient of mystical experiences that revealed some degree of the nature of existence, the mind, and consciousness. Sharing what I have received with the world is an absolute joy. As I share, still more is revealed.

I will leave it up to you to determine whether what I share here is of value in your life. To me, the value of *the principle* is directly proportionate to how its application improves the quality of my daily experience. You might apply the same metric in your evaluation of this book and *the principle* that it reveals.

Having said much about what *The Genesis Code* is, let me say what it is not. Although this book does contain pertinent accounts of revelatory experience, it's not a memoir. *The Genesis Code* is not born of New Age thinking, Gnosticism, Kabbala, Hinduism, Buddhism, Taoism, or any other ism. Simply put, this book reveals a fundamental *principle* found in the book of Genesis—period.

To reiterate, if you want to fundamentally improve the quality of your life by releasing the internal patterns and divisions that no longer serve you, *The Genesis Code* is for you.

The code has always been in Genesis just waiting for us. I couldn't see it until it was shown to me. If you could use some help decoding Genesis, as I certainly did, this book may be of service to you.

Tools for Success

Mindset

As Jesus so often warned, "To those who have the eyes to see and the ears to hear, more will be given; and to those who have not, more still will be taken away." If you understand the teachings and apply them to your life, more still will you benefit, deeper still will you understand. But if you misperceive the teachings, even greater will be your confusion as a result of the teachings. We are wise to proceed carefully. This book does everything possible to prepare your eyes to see. If you practice *the principle* with complete honesty to the depth of your soul, the benefits will astonish you!

Having the eyes to see and the ears to hear largely means having an honest, open heart, and the ability to set aside preconceived notions which can skew, fog, or block understanding entirely. Therefore, to get the most out of *The Genesis Code*, prepare to set aside strongly held beliefs, at least as you read, and center yourself in honesty. Seeing the meaning behind the code does not require a giant leap of faith, but it will help to be fully open to the teachings as they come. You can always reject them later, if you like.

The Transparent English Bible

As this book is dedicated to exposing the essential teachings of Genesis, finding the most reflective English translation of the original Hebrew text was essential. To my surprise, I found the various popular translations lack the precision, subtlety, and depth of the original Hebrew. Those translations tend to gloss over seemingly non-essential information, that, as it turns out, is helpful to proper conveyance of the code.

Although the code, as I saw it, lines up very well even with modern English biblical translations, certain assumed meanings, vagaries, and discrepancies within those translations can mislead readers. To truly verify the code, I was keen to find a translation that more accurately reflected the original Hebrew.

To my astonishment, a new translation came out just a few months after the code appeared to me. I was unaware of that sweet serendipity until a meditation student of mine, Linda LaTores, aware of my search, sent me a copy of *The Book of Genesis: A New Translation from the Transparent English Bible* by James D. Tabor. When I opened it to Genesis 1 and began reading, inspiration welled up. This was the translation I had been looking for!

Not wanting to distort the text to fit preconceived notions, I felt it best to include all of the chapters that pertain to *The Genesis Code*, exactly as Professor Tabor translated them. Strict copyright laws, of course, prevent that possibility, unless granted permission by the author. I reached out to Dr. Tabor requesting full use of those chapters. I was surprised when I received a warm reply from him, not only granting me the rights to the full text, but also to the notes that support the text.

Dr. Tabor's translation is highly detailed and carries with it an innovative system of notes, superscript, capitalization, bolding, italics, and spacing to convey additional information. When you get to the translated text starting in Part 2, please refer to the Tabor Translation Reader's Guide at the end of this section to understand the translation as it's meant to be. With my greatest hopes exceeded, and with Dr. Tabor's blessing, I include his translation here.

Many passages will be repeated throughout the book, so to avoid clutter, I will remove the notes that are not immediately germane to what is being indicated at the time. You will notice the numbering for the notes in my commentary are not in numerical order. The aim is to easily compare the notes in my commentary with the notes at the end of Dr. Tabor's book. There are also broad spacings in the translation meant to signal the reader to pause and reflect. I have removed them from the incorporated text in my chapters, but you can find them in the full translation at the back of the book.

As the content related to the code centers primarily on just three chapters, I highly encourage anyone interested in the full book of Genesis to purchase Dr. Tabor's book for the other 47 chapters. His true-to-source translation contains the most captivating English conveyance of the book of Genesis to date. I can't recommend it highly enough!

The Book of Genesis, by James D. Tabor Amazon link for print or Kindle: https://www.amazon.com/dp/B08GGB8X84

The Tabor Translation Reader's Guide

Italic Type indicates words **not** in the Hebrew but supplied for smoother English style

Names or terms for God such as ELOHIM, YHVH, or ADONAI are indicated in all CAPS

Explanatory footnotes are at the bottom of the page and indicated by a superscript number[2]

Words in **bold italics** indicate special emphasis in the Hebrew

Masculine[m] Feminine[f] Singular[s] Plural[p] Causitive[c] and the Definite[d] article are indicated by these tiny superscript letters

These special "white spaces" are in the original Hebrew manuscripts, indicating a break in thought or an emphasis of a section of text

Chapter 3:14 And YHVH ELOHIM said to the Naḥash, "Because you have done this, cursed *are* you above every animal, and above every living thing of the field; upon your belly you will walk, and dust you will eat, all the days of your life[f]. **15** And hatred I will place between you and between the woman, and between your seed and between her seed;[1] *he* will strike[2] you—*on the* head, and *you* will strike him—*on the* heel." **16** To the woman he said, "Causing to be many—I will *surely* cause to be many!—your distress[3] and your pregnancy; in distress you will bring forth sons, and toward your man[4] *will be* your craving, and *he* will rule with[5] you." **17** And to Adam[6] he said, "Because you hearkened to[7] the voice of your woman, and you ate from the tree that I charged you saying, 'You shall not eat from it,' cursed *is* the soil on account of you. In distress[8] you will eat *of* it all the days of your life[f]; **18** and thorn and thistle it will sprout for you, and you will eat the plant of the field. **19** In the sweat of your two nostrils you will eat bread, until you return to the soil, for from it you were taken; for dust you *are*, and to dust you will return."

---

[1] Or "offspring," Heb *zera'* normally refers to male "seed," but can refer to female reproduction (Gen 16:10; Lev 12:2).
[2] Or "bruise."
[3] Or "sorrow," same word as v. 17b.
[4] Heb *'ish*.
[5] I.e., with regard to.
[6] Heb *'adam*, *soul*-man, without the article, probably here the proper name.
[7] Lit "heard to."
[8] Or "sorrow," same word as v. 16.

Online Resources

When I address related material found elsewhere in the Bible, I include quotes from the New International Version (NIV), as it consistently ranks highly on lists of the most popular and accurate modern biblical translations. If you do not have a physical copy of the NIV, I recommend using Biblegateway.com or Biblehub.com to verify the passages from the NIV.

When using these websites, you can enter the book, chapter, and verse number as I have formatted it, and the website will instantly take you to the directed text. It doesn't get any easier!

If you would like to read an entire chapter to gain context of biblical quotes, just remove the numbers after the colon. For example, if I indicate Matthew 5:14-16, and you want to see not only those verses but the entire chapter, then you would only enter Matthew 5 into the search field on BibleGateway.com or Biblehub.com.

You will note that there are bracketed, colored links in the text on Biblegateway.com and Biblehub.com that I have not included in my book. I have removed those largely for esthetic purposes. Those links take you to the notes at the bottom of the page of BibleGateway and/or BibleHub, where you can see alternative word translations. Unless those alternative words more accurately reflect the code than the word choice of the translator, I generally do not include them in the text. I highly recommend clicking on each of those notes to see the alternatives.

Part 1

Mystical Revelations

The transformative *principle* of Genesis has been hidden in plain sight for thousands of years. I read Genesis time and again and missed it each and every time. Eventually, I did see it, but in fairness, I can't take credit for the find. For reasons that I cannot fathom, the code came to me through a lifelong series of dreams and mystical experiences.

Although an accumulation of such experiences spanning four decades prepared me for the revelation of the code, primarily only a handful of those experiences provide the essential foundation required to recognize the hidden code in Genesis. Part 1 shares those formative experiences to help you develop the eyes to see the code for yourself.

Chapter 1 outlines the first mystical experience, a dream of Jesus that set the direction and momentum of my life that ultimately allowed for the realization of the code.

Chapter 2 explores a direct experience of the unifying force that many people might call God. This experience conveys the fundamental mindset required to both perceive the code and to employ *the principle* that the code reveals.

Chapter 3 explores the geometry of unified consciousness. This geometry will allow your mind to more effectively intuit and embody *the principle* of Genesis.

Chapter 4 reveals how I was shown the code. This chapter will help you to shed unhelpful beliefs and biases. If allowed to persist unchecked, those forces may prevent you from seeing the full ramifications of the code and *the principle* that it conveys.

As I stated, Part 1 is dedicated to developing the eyes to see, which means developing the proper foundational understanding. Developing a foundational understanding will not only help you to recognize the code, but to embody the principle that it points to in your daily life. Without embodiment, the code is just another bit of trivial mental clutter to consider. At least to me, embodiment is incomparably more rewarding!

Chapter 1

First Contact

My first mystical experience occurred when I was about eight years old. It came to me after a failed attempt to convert my parents to Christianity.

An older boy informed the rest of the neighborhood children that his mother was teaching Bible Study on Wednesday evenings. We were warned that we had better attend or we would surely go to Hell. We attended.

Gradually, over a period of months, the teacher indoctrinated us to believe we were shepherds of the Lord. We were told Jesus wanted us to convert our parents to Christianity to save them from eternal hellfire. Fully believing the teacher, I was determined to convert my parents.

When I returned home that evening, I asked my parents if we could discuss religion, and to my surprise, they agreed. We met in the dining area after dinner for our discussion. As my father knew much more about religion than my mother, the discussion was primarily between the two of us.

He opened the conversation by asking if I believed God was the source of love—I did. He then asked if I thought it loving to send someone to Hell for not being Christian. This question stimulated feelings of uncertainty within me. To make his point, he asked me to imagine myself as God. He then asked if I would send anyone to Hell for not being Christian.

"Of course not," I said.

He then asked if I would love or respect a God that would send people to Hell merely for being non-believers. Upon careful consideration, I realized not only would I not respect that God, I would hate that God. My father then explained there were many people in far-off lands who might never hear of Christianity, and therefore, would have no ability to choose it as their religion. It seemed wrong to me that they should go to Hell merely because they lacked information.

He then explained that other religions also claim only those who worship *their* way are spared the fires of Hell. I was confused. How can multiple religions make the same claim? I realized either we are all going to Hell or that particular doctrine is false. In either case, if God operated by this policy, in my opinion, he was not worthy of respect.

We opened our Bibles and began comparing verses. Upon comparison, he pointed out the differences between the three Bible translations, and how, from those variances, different conclusions could be reached. He then directed my attention to the differences found in the resurrection stories as documented in Matthew, Mark, Luke, and John. I was shocked to see how drastically different they were, even within a single version of the Bible.

The four accounts of that pivotal moment are so inconsistent that none of them seemed trustworthy. The stories range from the supernatural to the mundane, from entering the tomb to remaining outside. At most, only one of those accounts could reflect the actual events at the tomb, but there was no way to know which, if any.

I wondered how much of Jesus' life story was likewise distorted. The obvious discrepancies cast doubt in my mind about the reliability of Jesus' chroniclers, and thus the entire Jesus narrative. Deep down, I still felt there was an incredibly important kernel of truth held in The Holy Bible; but what that truth was exactly, I could not identify.

As we concluded our discussion, my father confided that he didn't think anyone knew the truth about Jesus or God. He then stressed if I really wanted to know the truth about God, I would need to be very honest, keep an open mind, and keep searching.

I was fortunate that my father had studied the Bible and was willing to discuss the topic honestly and respectfully with me, even though I was just a child. Contrary to what one might assume, our conversation did not turn me away from the Bible; instead, it inspired me to take it more seriously. I realized I needed to remove my positive bias and to approach the book more honestly. Even after that talk, I still felt deeply drawn to the Christ narrative.

Shortly after that conversation, I received my first mystical experience. After going to bed one night, I awoke in a dream-state that felt infinitely more real and meaningful than ordinary reality, and I found a man lying on the floor in the middle of my bedroom.

Waking to a stranger in the room should terrify any child, but oddly, I felt no fear. I looked around and noticed the room was filled with a warm glow that seemed to beckon me toward him.

I got out of bed and approached from his left side. As I neared him, our eyes met. Looking into his eyes, it felt like I was being absorbed by infinite wells of wisdom, loving compassion, and profound sorrow. Instinctively, I knew this man was Jesus Christ. How I knew, I cannot precisely quantify—I just knew to the depth of my being.

He gazed into my eyes for a time and with a long, drawn-out voice said, "Help me." In my childhood innocence, I assumed he was asking me to help him up, so I grabbed his left wrist with both hands and with the strongest pull an eight-year-old me could muster, attempted to lift him onto his feet.

To my surprise, his arm deformed in my grip like a water-balloon. I looked down at his body and saw it was sagging. I realized he had no skeleton. Confused, I looked back into his eyes. After a moment, he slowly repeated, "Help me."

I awoke in tears, confused, and panicked, wanting to help but not knowing how, wanting to return to that dream but unable to do so. I had the same dream multiple times for a period of about six months. Each occurrence was exactly the same to the finest detail, a fact I remembered only upon waking. Within the dream, however, it always seemed as if it were the very first time.

The dream felt so meaningful that its memory followed me throughout my days; the words, "Help me" echoed in the back of my mind wherever I was. I became obsessed with unraveling the mystery of this dream.

All I really wanted was to help Jesus. The only problem: I had no idea what Jesus wanted of me. I felt tremendous frustration after each dream because I always awoke just moments before I received his answer.

Upon waking, I could remember the many times I had woken similarly confused. Frustration developed from a combination of confusion and the growing belief that I would never receive an answer. I was stuck in a dual loop of a repeating dream and emotional torment, desperately wanting to help but unable to.

"If only I could stay in the dream just a few more moments, I would have my answer," I thought.

Each night prior to sleep, I prayed to remain in that dream-state just a bit longer to hear Jesus' full request. For months my prayers seemed ineffectual, until one night, when I finally got the answer.

The dream was exactly the same as it had always been, but unexpectedly, at the instant where I always awoke, the moment where Jesus asks for help the second time, a surge of energy filled my body, anchoring me in the dream.

"How can I help you?" I asked.

Jesus looked straight into my eyes, and, after a pause, said, "Find my bones, for they are the core of my teaching. Most of what is written about me is untrue. Mankind has so twisted my teachings for selfish gain that little of the essence remains. What little remains is largely overlooked in the religious ritual and confusion. Find the essence of my teachings and give it back to the world. That is how you can help. Will you do this?"

Every cell in my body seemed to light up with inspiration. I knew that this was my life's purpose. "Yes," I said, "I will." With that promise, I awoke from the dream feeling a profound sense of relief. That was the last time I saw Jesus, and it was the beginning of a lifelong search for *the principle* of his teachings: the bones of Christ.

Because Jesus indicated that some small portion of the essence was accurately portrayed in The Holy Bible and because I had nowhere else to begin my search, I turned to scripture. In retrospect, it was an act of desperation, for deep in my bones, I knew that I would not realize the essential teachings by reading books or listening to authorities. How I would find it, I did not know, but somehow, I knew it would be revealed through my life experience.

Chapter 2

The Infinite

About fifteen years passed before I received any notable information relating to my promise to Jesus. In my early twenties, I finally made progress. I had just broken my ankle. The pain was excruciating, and I was trying to meditate myself beyond it. The intensity of the pain served to keep my mind fully present in the meditative endeavor. Instinctively, I felt I needed to forgive any negativity held against myself, other people, and life. Through a process of forgiveness, spontaneously, old memories arose within my mind to be seen and released from judgment.

At some point in the process, my perception of the physical world thinned, and I entered a timeless abyss that stimulated great fear. Somehow, I knew I needed to forgive that too. As the fear dissipated, so too did the experience of the dark abyss. I then experienced a profound unified being, and I realized that I was in the presence of the Infinite.

I sensed a palpable intelligence and power so perfect and loving that it defied language. The presence was utterly whole — Holy. In that instant, my language-limited, culturally conditioned, time-bound perception of the Infinite evaporated.

The Infinite began communicating with me outside of language through direct understanding. It seemed as though knowledge and experience entered my mind to be understood immediately, without thought, in ways that language cannot adequately convey. When I inquired about the nature of the Infinite, its answer, if forced into words, would be something like "There is no other."

I had read in the New Testament that God is the alpha and the omega. Alpha and omega are the first and last letters of the Greek alphabet. The meaning is that God is the beginning and the end, whole, complete, *all-that-is*, and so I understood I was in the presence of what a Christian might call "God."

A power resided in this presence that was incomprehensible, yet felt fully palpable. If this was God, it was entirely beyond what I had imagined when reading the Bible, for I encountered not a hint of judgment or wrath, qualities frequently ascribed to God in the Old Testament.

In a lot of ways, the experience of the Infinite is the opposite of those stories, for the Infinite is perfectly forgiving (knowing that there is nothing to forgive), nonjudgmental, and unconditionally loving. Its harmony is so complete that I did not feel judged in the least in its presence. Later, though, as I compared myself with the memory of perfect wholeness, my apparent imperfections stood glaringly forth.

This subsequent comparison was an erroneous formulation created by my conditioned mind and ego. I believe such harsh formulations have caused many religions to veer astray with their judgmental doctrines. Based on my experience, I can easily see how what may have originated in true communion with the Infinite could become a stifling judgmental outlook.

The experience of the Infinite is far more real than physical reality ever feels. Describing an experience of the Infinite is more difficult than explaining sight to a person who has never seen or smell to someone missing olfactory nerves. Despite the apparent futility, the desire to share has led to countless bumbling attempts.

Many differences have come to exist among human beings and their beliefs, but the most fundamental difference resides in beliefs about the nature of the Universe and of consciousness. Theologians have numerous theories of what God is, while scientists have myriad notions about the nature of the Universe.

Regardless of the particular belief or notion, they all come down to two primary perspectives. The first idea, generally embraced by spiritually minded individuals, holds that the Universe is conscious at its very foundation, and therefore everything is conscious. This notion is popularly called "panpsychism." The other main perspective, generally held in the scientific community, assumes that the Universe is made up of unconscious matter and therefore has no innate awareness.

The Infinite statement, "There is no other" indicates that there is no difference between the Infinite and what we think of as the Universe, and therefore no difference between the Infinite and ourselves.

The typical religious view of God differs from the way that I am using the word Infinite here. Religious leaders would typically see God as outside of physicality. Their perspective may be summarized as follows: there is God and then something other than God, which God created. This duality causes humans much confusion and disharmony.

The perspective of "no other" resolves the confusion once one's mind acclimates to the perspective. Let's explore the idea of panpsychism to help make that adjustment. Panpsychism is a perspective that I was entirely unfamiliar with until the experience with the Infinite revealed it to me through the assertion that there is no other.

These days panpsychism is a growing notion even in the scientific community, as all materialistic theories to date fail to account for consciousness in human beings and animals. The scientific community long resisted the idea that animals could be conscious, but ever-growing evidence suggests otherwise. For example, the great apes, elephants, dolphins, and even some birds like crows and magpies have demonstrated the capacity to recognize themselves in a mirror, plan for the future, and make tools to fulfill those plans. These abilities are all traits that we have ascribed to consciousness.

As we continue discovering that animals share capabilities we previously assumed were human-specific, we are forced to admit either that animals are conscious or that we do not understand what consciousness is. I suspect both are true: we are not the only conscious beings, and we don't understand what consciousness is. Maybe, just maybe, consciousness is inherent to all things within the Universe. Maybe consciousness is the Universe.

The problem with the materialist viewpoint, which asserts that consciousness is a by-product of material processes, is that it has no verifiable evidence as to what creates consciousness—where it comes from, or how it works, let alone what consciousness actually is. It seems human life revolves around consciousness, which is to say, even by scientific metrics, consciousness is absolutely fundamental to all experience. Maybe consciousness is what experiences as well as what is experienced. Maybe there is no other.

As important as the question of consciousness is, to date, the materialist view has utterly failed to make any headway. In all fairness, consciousness is something that science has not, as of yet, helped us to understand. If we are conscious beings, and if consciousness is central to every experience we have, then it means that science, relying exclusively on the materialist lens, has failed to provide us with any insight into our deeper nature. It might be time for science to give panpsychism its fair shake.

Maybe it's time we took off the blinders and stopped pretending that we understand ourselves, other animals, life, or the Universe. We might first admit that we don't know and that the materialist lens may be insufficient to the task before we can begin to see with fresh eyes.

What we do know is that consciousness is central to every single moment of our waking lives. Considering the pervasiveness of consciousness to all experience, one would think more scientists and more money would be flowing into that field than any other area of research. Even if it were a more popular, better funded field, until we surrender the materialist viewpoint, it's unlikely that consciousness will take its rightful place as the brave new frontier of research. Until then, we will likely remain ignorant of ourselves.

Chapter 3

The Face of God

As I said in the previous chapter, when I asked the Infinite about its nature, it replied "There is no other." In actual fact, "There is no other" is not what the Infinite conveyed, but my translation of what it conveyed, so as to make a complete sentence. What actually came through was "No other." What *no other* means is that everything that *is*, is the Infinite, which includes you and me. If there was anything within that experience that caused me torment, it was this concept.

I just could not wrap my head around the idea that, from the perspective of the Infinite, I was it. How is it possible that I could be one with *all-that-is* and not know it? How could I be perfectly whole when, in my own estimation, I was a bag of disharmony and confusion?

For years that question plagued me. Deep within I knew the perspective of the Infinite was true, but I could not understand how it could be true. I seemed unable to visualize the geometry that would allow for the wholeness of the Infinite experience.

After the experience of the Infinite, getting the right question became my aim. From that encounter, I understood that sequential thinking was unhelpful, so I abandoned the time-based approach. Still, no answers came.

To get a sense of the Infinite, I understood I needed to consider things through the lens of *potential* rather than material existence. I understood that I needed to look for a seamless *unity* rather than separation. Still, my mind failed me.

Roughly two decades passed before I gained clarity on that question, again through mystical experience. One night, while watching TV with my family, I unexpectedly found myself immersed in a visionary state that revealed the geometry of the Infinite. As this geometry will likely help others' minds skirt much of the confusion that I experienced, I want to share it here.

Although I am not capable of fully articulating what I experienced, this model enables the mind to see things in a seamless way that fits the description "no other." Most importantly, this seamless perspective provides a key to understanding *the principle* found in the creation mythology of Genesis.

In our model, we will begin with the idea that consciousness is the basis of *all-that-is*, as described in Chapter 2. Let's imagine that this foundational consciousness has no real form or apparent substance. We can use basic mathematics to fulfill that aim by assigning the fundamental consciousness a value of zero in our model. To remind the reader that zero in our model is conscious, I will refer to it variously as "Zero" and as the "Witness."

In our timeless model, in accordance with the statement "no other," we will say that Zero (the Witness) understands that it has no predecessor, for without time there is no before or after. The Witness is fully open consciously, which means it is open to all potential, including the possibility of forgetting its own nature. Its unbounded openness allows even the potential of limitation, such as seeming to have specific experiences, just as humans have dreams that can seem quite real. For the Infinite, these dream-like states are continuous speculations about its nature, which we humans might best understand as holograms—two dimensional images that only appear to be three-dimensional.

While most humans have only encountered holograms in sci-fi books and movies, we all have dreams, which we also experience as three dimensional when they are, in fact, contained within our own minds. However, if the Universe is a hologram, to human beings the experience of those "dreams" is reality, for we are within and of the mind of the Witness.

Here, some geometry will help us further explore the conceptual and dimensional projections of the Witness. Remember, in our model the Witness always sums to zero. Because the nature of the Witness is and always will be zero, every potential that it sees is instantly counterbalanced by the opposite potential. For example, the idea of "Is" would be balanced by the opposite idea "Isn't," while "Am" is balanced by "Am not." With these counterbalanced polarities in mind, the Witness speculates that it exists and does not exist simultaneously.

So, to get a visual sense of the witnessing process, let's imagine that these two primary categories of concepts (positive and negative) constitute two opposite poles, much like a magnet. Because the two concepts are interdependently opposing, the positive and negative forces both push away from the center and curve toward each other, creating circular fields of energy. Now

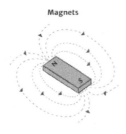

Magnets

Figure 1: Magnetic energy flows

imagine infinite arching energies streaming between the poles, each representing different positive and negative ideas of self. See Figure 1. The combined effect of these countless streams of energy produces the shape of a torus, which is a donut or ring shape. See Figure 2.

Note that the torus image in Figure 2 has been rendered with a large hole in the center to help us visualize the geometry. With that in mind, imagine that that hole is immeasurably or imperceptibly

Figure 2: Torus

small. I describe the hole as being immeasurably small because there is nothing that is actually outside of zero. To get any actual measurement, we require something other than that which is being measured for comparison.

To exemplify the point, imagine you, everyone, and everything you know exist inside a box. There is nothing outside of the box, and no one has ever been outside of it. In that scenario, you can't truly measure the box. With the inability to get outside of it, you can only measure the box relative to what is inside it, from your limited point of view. Without a broader perspective, which would require getting outside the box, you lack a precise means of measuring its actual size or anything within it. Effectively, the box's size is zero, as is everything within it, even if that does not seem to be the case.

Reminder: zero is the sum of both the hole and the arching streams of energy that make up the torus. The hole is obviously zero, while the positive and negative arching energies balance to zero.

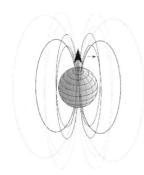

Figure 3: Sphere of tori

Next, let us imagine a sphere made up of multiple tori, like a planet, with charged poles at the top and bottom. See Figure 3. We could imagine that the pole at the top represents the positive polarity from which affirmative ideas like "I am" project, while the pole at the bottom represents the negative pole, which represents "I am not." The orderly idea of "I am" curves toward its interdependent opposite. The countless one-dimensional arching strands of opposing speculative energies (the tori) combine to make up what might appear to be a smooth three-dimensional surface area.

When we remember that the Infinite is continuously creating holographic projections, and that projections are composed of other projections, we can visualize zooming in on an individual projection, an arching strand, and see that it is beaded together by comparatively smaller spheres, which are also made up of strands of energy born of dual interdependent ideas, ad infinitum. So, whether we zoom in or zoom out, each torus composed of holographic projections appears to be three-dimensional.

Thus, we can visualize the Witness' continuous projections as three-dimensional structures not unlike our own bodies, which are made up of countless microscopic cells—each a witness, a center of perception, a dance of energy.

We can also, as I did during my vision, see infinite opposing concepts streaming from the Witness, creating a visual effect like a fountain of light pouring out of what looked surprisingly similar to the pupil of an eye.

And lastly, again based on my visionary experience, we could compare the Witness' continuous holographic projections to that of our universe, which is filled with galaxies, solar systems, planets, and stellar constellations.

So, we now have three seemingly holographic dimensions born of an unformed consciousness exploring itself through opposing ideas—our cells, our eyes, and our universe. Just a reminder—I am not a physicist. I am only conveying what I witnessed in a mystical state for the purpose of helping you view life as a unified field rather than a bunch of separate particles or random atomic bodies banging up against each other. If the model I offer here helps the mind to intuit the unified field of the Witness more clearly, then it serves its purpose.

Because our perception is time-bound, we humans see the spheres within spheres as a planned process devised by a creator. However, when viewed from the open perspective of the Witness, there is no past or future, only the present—it's a revelation, not a choice or a plan.

Interestingly, a popular scientific hypothesis called the "zero-energy universe" states the Universe has a total energy sum of zero. How is that possible, we might wonder. Well, if all of the positive energies are counterbalanced by negative energies, as is the case with atoms where proton counts (positive charges) match electron counts (negative charges), there is net zero energy, which is to say the sum of the energy of the Universe is zero.

A well-known criticism of this hypothesis comes from a quantum cosmologist, Christopher Isham. Isham suggests that "ontic seeding" is required to conjure the positive and negative energy in the first place. The key word "ontic" is a philosophical term which indicates physical, real, or factual existence.

Isham's criticism presumes that matter is, in fact, a thing. If the reality that we perceive is more akin to a hologram born of conscious zero, then his argument is zeroed out, pardon the pun.

How would we know whether what we call reality is a hologram or not? Our intuition reinforces the way that our minds are accustomed to framing reality, making it very difficult to determine reality's true nature.

Honestly, I am unsure how science could ever determine one way or the other because the current scientific method requires comparisons to make conclusions. If scientists had a way of getting outside of reality to take a comparative measurement, then they might be able to tell us a little something about this question. Alas, getting outside of reality seems impossible, at least according to our current understanding of physics.

This brings us back to the witnessing Zero. From the perspective of the Witness, there is no other, and therefore all that is perceived and that which perceives it is no-thing. In a way it is fair to say that you are an eye of the Witness. I am an eye of the Witness. Everything is the Witness. We are all witnessing.

How does this mystical experience and the theory of panpsychism that we discussed in Chapter 2 make any sense? Are we to assume that a rock is just as intelligent as a human being? That assumption is not required if we recognize that consciousness and intelligence are not synonymous.

According to Merriam-Webster, "intelligence" is defined as follows:

(1) : the ability to learn or understand or to deal with new or trying
situations : reason also : the skilled use of reason

(2) : the ability to apply knowledge to manipulate one's environment or to think abstractly as measured by objective criteria (such as tests)

Merriam-Webster defines "consciousness" as follows:

1 a : the quality or state of being aware especially of something within oneself
b : the state or fact of being conscious of an external object, state, or fact

Essentially, intelligence is the capacity to juggle data, whereas consciousness, at least as I mean it, is the capacity to perceive, to witness.

Assuming our definitions of intelligence equals the capacity to juggle or manipulate data and consciousness as the ability to perceive, let's look at some non-human life to develop the notion a bit further.

An insect might not be able to juggle much data, but they do perceive. In fact, the Cambridge Declaration on Consciousness, signed by prominent neuroscientists in 2012, states unequivocally that "humans are not unique in possessing the neurological substrates that generate consciousness. Non-human animals, including all mammals and birds, and many other creatures, including octopuses, also possess these neural substrates."

I suspect that as more studies come in, it will become clearer that all animals have some very basic consciousness. According to what I have seen through mystical experience, even an atom has a fundamental awareness of being. An atom may not have the various senses and ability to think like you or I do, but it may be fundamentally aware of its existence.

Whether we believe all is conscious at a fundamental level or not, it will help to remember the concept of panpsychism and the unified nature of being when we get to the creation mythology of Genesis a bit later. Moving forward, I will use Zero, the Witness, and the Infinite interchangeably. Witness is employed to indicate the fundamental perceptual nature of being, while Infinite is used to indicate its immeasurability.

Chapter 4

In Plain Sight

One night, during the same year as the occurrence of the mystical experience I playfully call "The Face of God," I was immersed in the last of the extraordinary experiences relevant to this book. On that particular night, I simply could not fall asleep.

My body tossed and turned for hours without a single thought in my mind. Finally, at about 3 a.m., I entered a twilight state between dream and wakefulness. My body surged with energy—I knew I was entering a mystical experience.

There, in my mind's eye, was my opened Bible, the pages rapidly flipping backward from end to beginning, eventually stopping at Genesis 1, the opening text of the Hebrew Bible. The key text of Genesis was highlighted in yellow. The pages then slowly flipped forward, highlighting as it went. Instantly, I understood the highlighted text was a hidden code that revealed *the principle* of Jesus' teachings, which at age eight, I had promised to rediscover and share with the world.

The visionary state lasted for an indeterminate period, but once it finished, my body relaxed, and I fell into a deep sleep. When I awoke to my alarm clock a few hours later, the vision was still fresh in my mind. I rushed into my office to compare what I was shown with what was written in my various Bible translations.

I turned to Genesis 1. To my great astonishment, there before me, in plain sight, was the code, embedded in the place I least expected to find it. The meaning was so obvious that I wondered how I had missed it before. After all, I had read Genesis time and again over the years, disliking it more with each reading. Clearly, in my youth, I did not have the "eyes to see." I could now see that Jesus' teachings, if true, must have rested on the hidden *principle* within Genesis.

Now, let's consider Jesus and his followers. As we discussed in the Introduction, Jesus is quoted as stating to his disciples (as recounted in the books of Matthew, Mark, and Luke) that, to the masses, he only spoke in parables to hide the truth from them. A follower is unlikely to understand what they are not yet prepared to understand. One must learn to count before one can add or subtract. Based on the many inconsistencies between the four canonical accounts of Jesus' life in Matthew, Mark, Luke, and John, I suspect that whoever wrote those stories did not have the foundation to understand the code and were likely never direct students of Jesus. The vast majority of biblical scholars agree on this last point.

While researching for this book, I found that the oldest extant gospel is Mark, upon which, it seems, the other gospels, Matthew, Luke, and John are based. The vast majority of New Testament scholars believe Mark's Gospel was written around 70 CE, some four decades after the reported death of Jesus.

As proof of the late date, they point to details within Mark about the First Roman-Jewish War as well as mention of the battle within the walls of Jerusalem as the Romans lay siege. The author of Mark, whoever that was, was not actually a disciple of Jesus. The books Matthew, Luke, and John, written decades after Mark, similarly appear to have been authored by non-witnesses to the events of Jesus' life.

If the biblical accounts of Jesus' life are hearsay, based on incorrect understandings and the desire to popularize a growing faith, how can we trust them? If I am being honest, I can't. But, as the chapters to come will demonstrate, Genesis contains the transformative *principle*, the truth, that many of us are seeking.

No matter how many people teach *the principle*, if they are teaching it honestly, it is the same *principle*. With that in mind, my allegiance is to *the principle*, not to any specific teacher, including Jesus.

The principle is universal and primary, analogous to mathematics. No one owns math. *The principle* is not Jesus' *principle*, nor is it *the principle* of whoever may have encoded it into Genesis. It's just *the principle*.

The principle is so simple that once seen, it cannot be unseen. That said, it is a bit subtle at first, due to how counterintuitive it is. However, with repeated exposure, the brain opens up to it. When embraced, that truth will begin to unravel the prison of the mind and reveal a greater depth within us than we might have thought possible.

Do not expect to move mountains, walk on water, or raise the dead; at least, that has not been my experience thus far. If *the principle* offends in any way, please know that is not my intention, although offense may be an instinctive response to that which threatens comforting beliefs.

I've not found comfort-beliefs to be compatible with *the principle*. Working with *the principle*, you, like me, may find that you no longer need comfort-beliefs. So long as you abide by *the principle*, you will see that you are strong enough to handle the emotional vicissitudes of life directly, without need of the emotional insulation that comfort-beliefs offer. But be forewarned, once you truly see what I delineate here, try as you may, you can't unsee it.

Part 2

Developing the Eyes to See

Before we define the code, let's talk about what it is not. Genesis, much like creation mythologies around the world, presents many layers of information, but only one of those layers represents the code. A reader who is unable to parse out the various layers will almost certainly not see it.

With the aim of developing the eyes to see, Part 2 will analyze and parse the layers of Genesis that do not represent the code.

To accomplish that aim, in Chapter 5, we will familiarize ourselves with the power of creation mythology and the common elements of creation mythology found around the world.

In Chapter 6, we look specifically at Genesis through the lens of creation mythology, as we learned to do in Chapter 5, so that we can become conscious of the layers of Genesis.

In Chapter 7, we explore the many essential qualities and oddities of Genesis. Were it not for the peculiarities of Genesis, there would be no code. Being attentive to the unusual aspects of the text will help develop our eyes to see the code when we begin Part 3.

In Chapter 8, we examine how our ideas about the nature of God and reality may distort our perception of the code. I also point out the traps of blind belief so that we can begin to see through them and discover an innate, natural sense of the Infinite.

Chapter 5

The Power of Creation Mythology

By some means that I cannot fathom, the code has survived intact for thousands of years in written form and possibly much longer in oral form. Its integrity is astounding when we consider the many factors that serve to hide the code in plain sight and the many steps along the path where it could have been lost entirely.

Nearly every ancient culture found around the world has a distinct creation mythology. Although these stories vary widely from culture to culture, regardless of the form they take, they tend to share certain elements that help ensure the survival of the societies that embrace them. As we will be engaging with the creation myth of Judaism, we are wise to understand these common elements, for they will help us to overcome any biases that we may have for or against them. The exercise of purging our biases is requisite to developing the eyes to see and appreciate the code.

Human beings, unlike most other animals, lack fang, fur, and claw, so our survival depends heavily upon cultural cohesion. Although group belonging plays a large role in human well-being even in the most technologically advanced of countries, peoples who live more primitively rely upon group cohesion to survive more than those living in the world of high technology.

On one level, creation stories are survival tools without which human beings might not have survived long enough to have entered the age of science. Ironically, once in the cushy age of science, we may find it easy to dismiss the creation stories of our ancestors as being silly and unnecessary superstitions that should be done away with for the betterment of humanity.

For the modern, usually secular mind, the combination of science, philosophy, and political ideology may serve similar functions to mythology. Whether those elements achieve the same degree of group cohesion and long-term survivability is uncertain, but the question is under increasing debate as our societies lose apparent social, economic, and ecological stability at an increasing rate.

Although we might feel tempted to do so, we are wise not to take a shallow or dismissive view of creation mythology. Doing that will cause us to overlook the deeper elements within creation mythology, ones that might prove vital to our long-term survival. With an eye for detail, let's look at the main elements common to most creation stories to get an understanding of their function.

The first element common to many creation myths around the world is the supernatural, usually in the form of a creator or creators. The supernatural element provides shared targets of worship for the society, a common highest value. Whether the creator is one being or many appears less relevant than does the communal agreement of the people to respect or worship that being or those beings.

Generally, the supernatural element represents polytheism, the worship of multiple gods. Polytheism is said to be found in native cultures worldwide. In Japan, Shintoism is often thought to be an example of polytheism because it claims a distinct spirit or deity for just about everything. According to Shintoism, the Kami (Deity) exists in all things in nature and the whole of the Universe.

If we look deeper at cultures that appear to be polytheistic, what we typically find is actually pantheism, which is the belief that the Universe is the expression of the divine, or henotheism, which is the belief that multiple lower gods are the expression of or under an overarching singular Deity that is in everything.

Take for example the Lakota people of the Great Plains of the United States, who are often thought to be polytheistic for their belief in nature spirits. They also believe in Wakan Tanka, which is translated as "The Great Spirit." Wakan Tanka, according to the Lakota belief, is the sacredness in all things. The Great Spirit holds the Universe and the deities together.

Another religion of the East, Hinduism, is commonly thought of as polytheistic, when it too may be pantheistic or henotheistic. In Hinduism, everything is considered an expression of the divine, but within the divine there are many deities. So long as the society as a whole is open to the idea that everyone and everything is an expression of the divine, social cohesion can be maintained.

Monotheism, which is the worship of a singular deity, is historically speaking, a rather new concept, and is mostly associated with modern Christianity, Judaism, and Islam. Even so, much of what is considered monotheism is arguably henotheism.

For example, Muslims and Jews tend to argue that Christianity is not monotheism, but henotheism, due to the Christian belief that God is trinitarian in nature, composed of the Father, the Son, and the Holy Spirit. Henotheism holds that multiple deities are expressions of one divine essence, which is how Hindus feel about God. The only difference is the number of representatives of God. In Christianity, there are three in one, if you discount the angels, whereas in Hinduism, there are innumerable gods in one.

In any case, certainly a range of disparate religious beliefs exists across different societies, and many of these religious social structures have existed for thousands of years. It seems that as long as the majority of people within each society accept the common highest value, be it the worship of multiple gods, an overarching God with expressions as lower gods, or a singular God that is entirely independent of physicality, the shared belief supports social cohesion.

Belief in a common highest value appears to have been and may still be essential to the long-term survival of societies worldwide. The supernatural narrative provided that common value. It seems that the commonly shared value and the sense of meaning that the supernatural provides has been the primary benefit, but there are other benefits as well.

The supernatural element of mythology provides the easy answers to inquiries about the origins of the people, homeland, planet, or the Universe. For example, the creation myth of the Lenape peoples of North America depicts the earth as being held up on the back of a giant turtle, whereas the Hindu myth says giant elephants hold up the earth.

These stories satiated people's curiosity, at least until science proved them inadequate. Without science, these stories were all that we had to answer the unanswerable questions. Consider that leaders attract a following because they appear confident. To the masses, it seems, a leader who says "I don't know" is unappealing even when "I don't know" is often the honest answer.

Regardless of how clever a creation story is, it can never truly satisfy a mind determined to understand the cause of existence. Individuals who openly question the story are often considered outliers and are sometimes ostracized from the group for not worshipping properly. Outliers aside, mythological answers to the questions of origin seem to satisfy most children, which somewhat spares elders from the many questions that cannot be answered. If you've raised highly inquisitive children, you might sympathize.

A key benefit to creation stories is their centrality in establishing and sustaining social norms. In the Kojiki "Records of Ancient Matters," the Japanese creation myth, for example, there are two gods who together create the Japanese islands. One God is male (Izanagi) and the other female (Izanami). In their marriage ceremony, the female inappropriately takes the initiative and addresses the male first. This action runs against ancient Japanese cultural norms, wherein the male was required to address the female first, because the masculine energy is considered assertive like a penis, while the feminine energy is categorized as receptive like a vagina.

The story says that their first offspring was born deformed as a result of the faux pas. To correct the issue, they had to redo the marriage ceremony, being sure that the man addressed the woman first. This creation story seems to reinforce a social protocol, in which men were expected to lead.

Without the glue that social norms provide, it seems a society cannot hold together under the pressure of primitive life, which requires clear separation of roles and labor between the sexes, age groups, and sometimes between classes. Effectively, the division of labor is cooked into the stories, where men play a certain role and carry certain responsibilities, and women play another role and carry other responsibilities. Taken as a whole, this strategy works regardless of how each particular tribe allots the responsibilities.

Besides providing a shared highest value, answering origin questions, and protecting cultural norms, many creation myths include justifications for a people's right to the land that they occupy. Some stories take it further by justifying the people's right to take land from or enslave other, "less godly" people.

The forceful acquisition of lands and resources is an ugly tendency to be sure, but it is common to many other forms of life, not just humans. The difference between humans and other animals is that humans seem to have a need to create narratives to quell consciences. Creation stories, in some cases, serve to justify what might otherwise not be justifiable to the conscience.

To be fair, certain religious beliefs have the opposite effect, barring people from such aggressive actions. For example, the idea that all humans are created equal, which is an integral belief of Christianity, helped fuel the movements to end slavery and provide equal rights under the law regardless of skin color or gender.

Beyond these commonalities, creation myths worldwide also tend to explain the causes of sickness and death absent a scientific understanding of such things, and how to be in healthy communion with the deities, which are often thought to be, or at least represent, the flora and fauna of the environment. Creation myths also teach morality and ethics, songs, genealogies, laws, and semi-historical accounts, which is to say, accounts very loosely based on true stories.

To interpret mythology merely through the lens of scientific fact would be to miss its many layers and purposes, purposes that were essential to the survival of the tribes at the time of the myth's creation. Although much of the content in creation stories bears little or no apparent relevance to modern life, these accounts may yet contain elements that prove helpful or necessary to modern humans, elements that science is ill-equipped to provide.

In the modern world, much debate remains about the value of creation stories and the human tendency to embrace religious narratives. The debate is carried on among four main groups that frame the stories in distinct but often predictable ways.

The first group consists of fundamentalist believers who hold that the stories convey factual accounts of creation, a view that is almost without exception at odds with scientific findings.

The second party is characterized by the claim that scientific views supersede religious narratives, which are dismissed as superstition. We can refer to them as the "New Atheists." They do not consider that the tendency for humans to create religious narratives might be instinctive. We can see that these first two voices are categorically opposed, and I would suggest that neither will aid in our purposes here.

The third group covertly fits under the umbrella of believers, those who interpret their sacred stories as metaphors meant to convey values necessary for a healthy society. This sociological stance, if pressed, often pulls away to reveal that those who hold it do in fact believe in a supernatural deity. We might refer to these people as lay believers.

Finally, a smaller, growing group within the scientifically minded community argues that there may be real biological drives for the religious perspective. They suggest that we should not rush to judgment on the religious tendency, which may be a requirement for a healthy society.

These scientifically minded explorers argue that without religion, materialistic ideology will fill the void and may cause greater problems than religion does. Their most commonly cited example of materialist ideology filling the void is what some have called "identity politics," a contemporary tendency to align without question with categorical divisions like political parties, sexual orientation, skin color, class, et cetera, intolerantly, in the name of virtue. The famous psychologists Carl Jung and Dr. Jordan B. Peterson share this scientifically-minded perspective.

According to Dr. Peterson, a proponent of Jungian Psychology, any idea that cannot be questioned is like a virus that spreads to any person who is open to the idea. If the ideological virus spreads too far and wide, it will inevitably result in tyranny or a total collapse of society.

Modern societies are stuck, it seems, between the forces of religious ideology and secular ideology. If left unchecked this tension will certainly lead to a worldwide collapse of the liberal values that inspired the modern world as we know it. A growing number of people would openly cheer that outcome. They assume without evidence that what comes after the collapse will be an improvement. We are wise to note that there has never been a sustainable society based on materialistic ideology.

There is another way, an unseen path, which is encoded in Genesis. On the surface, *the principle* may appear religious, but when understood to any depth, we can see that *the principle* is neither religious, materialistic, nor idealistic in nature. *The principle* is another creature entirely.

Chapter 6

Genesis Creation Mythology

Chapter 5 provided an overview of common mythological elements to prepare our eyes to view Genesis 1-3 through the lens of mythology. Here we examine Genesis through that lens to see which of those layers it contains.

To help you develop the eyes to see, I will indicate many of the elements that are not the code. You might use those hints as means of narrowing down what you think the code might be. As the chapters to come will demonstrate, almost nothing that people think of as important or argue over in Genesis 1-3 is the code.

Genesis opens with an anthropomorphized supernatural deity that precedes the existence of the Universe and then speaks the Universe, the sky, the earth, the waters, the land, and the living beings into existence. The creative process is said to occur over a period of six days, with the seventh day dedicated to rest.

The seventh day, called the Sabbath, was used to mandate that the Jewish people pray, rest, and reflect every Saturday, which is certainly good for physical and psychological health. The healthy practice of the Sabbath is not the code.

Among other things, the first three chapters of Genesis also serve to educate the reader about the relationship between humans and the Infinite. To that end, in Genesis 1, we are introduced to the almighty creator. In Genesis 2, we are told of the loving relationship between the creator and humanity. In Genesis 3, we are shown the rift that occurred between humanity and the creator.

These stories convey the idea that human beings have the potential to heal this rift and thereby be accepted by God. The Jews believe people fall into Gehenna (Hell) due to unatoned for sin. Instead of focusing on sin, Judaism emphasizes doing good deeds (mitzvot.) During the messianic era, which, according to most Jewish sects, has not arrived as of yet, one can be forgiven and accepted to usher in the age of universal peace.

The first overt description of sin is found in Genesis 4:3-7, when Cain makes an unfit sacrifice to God:

> Now Abel kept flocks, and Cain worked the soil. 3 In the course of time Cain brought some of the fruits of the soil as an offering to the Lord. 4 And Abel also brought an offering—fat portions from some of the firstborn of his flock. The Lord looked with favor on Abel and his offering, 5 but on Cain and his offering he did not look with favor. So Cain was very angry, and his face was downcast. 6 Then the Lord said to Cain, "Why are you angry? Why is your face downcast? 7 If you do what is right, will you not be accepted? But if you do not do what is right, sin is

crouching at your door; it desires to have you, but you must rule over it."

In these short few passages lies the idea that virtue, practiced via good behavior, will allow us to be accepted by God. The inverse, sin, which, according to Jewish thinking is doing what is not good in God's estimation, means not being accepted by God. Upon these few passages lies the basis of the Jewish system of atonement that is embodied in detail in Exodus, Leviticus, Numbers, and Deuteronomy. This distinction between what God does and does not accept is not the code.

Genesis 2 claims man was created before woman and that woman was created from the body of the first man. This idea has informed cultural teachings that women should follow men. Further, in Genesis 3, when the man follows the woman, the result is a fall from God's grace. This has led to the teaching that men should not follow women. The teachings regarding who should follow whom is not the code.

We can still see this type of chauvinism in certain sects of Judaism that separate the sexes in many activities to avoid the moral and spiritual decay of men as a result of the sexual temptations of women. Most modern Jews no longer follow this teaching, with the primary exception of Orthodox Jews, as mentioned above.

In Genesis 2, the location of Eden is revealed as follows:

> **10** And a river goes out from Eden to make drink the garden, and from there it is separated and it becomes four heads. **11** The name of the one *is* Pishon; it goes around all the land of the Havilah, where there *is* gold, **12** and the gold of that land *is* good; there *are* bdellium and the onyx stone.

13 And the name of the second river *is* Gihon; it goes around all the land of Cush. **14** And the name of the third river *is* Hiddekel; it *is* the one walking east of Assyria. And the fourth river—it *is* Euphrates.

Like many creation myths, Genesis includes the location of creation. However, although the description of Eden includes geographical markers, specifically the four rivers, its location does not align with any modern geographical maps. Maybe the location of Eden was never meant to make sense.

Of course, these stories may come from oral traditions that stretch back tens of thousands of years, so maybe the rivers and lay of the land at that time differ from those now. As peoples migrate into new lands, they often take the names of their previous landmarks with them. So, it's also possible that the names of the landmarks were reused, like York and New York. In any case, the location of Eden is not the code.

Is God one or many, male or female? What about the age of creation? Genesis counts the generations born since God created Adam and Eve, which if correct, would indicate that the earth was less than 10,000 years old. That is not the code. Almost nothing of Genesis that people argue over is the code.

Chapter 7

The DNA of Genesis

Although Genesis shares many elements with creation stories found around the world, oddities at the macro and micro level of the story make it unique. Because our recognition of the code depends on us acknowledging some of those unusual aspects, we need an honest view of the essential qualities and uniqueness of Genesis to develop our eyes to see.

The first and most obvious oddity regarding Genesis 1-3 is not so much the text itself but how the Judeo-Christian religious community has biased public perception of the nature of the Infinite, making Genesis appear to say something not actually found in the text. Most creation mythologies around the world are either pantheistic or henotheistic. Remember, pantheism is the belief that everything is the Infinite. Henotheism, Greek for 'of one god,' is the worship of a single, supreme god while not denying the possible existence of other lower deities. It could also mean the

Infinite is one divine being that has many aspects represented as little 'g' gods.

Depending on an individual's subjective perspective, pantheism and henotheism could mean the same thing or very different things. It's sort of like the ancient Indian parable of the blind men and the elephant. With no concept of an elephant, they encounter one for the first time. One, feeling only the trunk, says it's a giant snake. Another, feeling a leg, argues that it's a tree trunk. Another feels only the tail and argues that it's a rope. Each partial experience of the whole is erroneously believed to be the whole.

Believers of henotheism may argue over which representation of the divine is the highest. For example, some Hindus claim Vishnu is the highest, while others argue for Shiva. They tend to at least accept the existence of the other deity. The difference is only which represents the highest value. The ancient Jews (pre-Moses) did not necessarily deny other gods. The first recorded "denial" of other gods is said to have come later through Moses, as is found in the book of Deuteronomy 4:35 (7th century B.C.E.)

> You were shown these things so that you might know that the Lord is God; besides him there is no other.

At first glance, the above text appears exclusionary, but when we reflect back on the infinite's statement in Chapter 2, we can see that it may instead be an all-inclusive statement. "There is no other" means that the Infinite is all things. In any case, to the consternation of many religious leaders, Genesis 1-3 depicts the Infinite in a pantheistic or henotheistic way, as seen in the text itself.

Despite the textual evidence in Genesis, religious leaders deny pantheism or henotheism, claiming instead that there is only one God who resides outside of creation, a belief that is known as monotheism. So that we do not argue over what the text shows, let's set aside any biases that we may have toward the story, at least temporarily. Doing so will allow us to explore with open hearts and clear eyes, qualities essential to seeing and applying *the principle* of the code.

Below are the two quotes from Genesis that contradict the monotheistic view. Please note the underlined keywords, for they provide the evidence we seek:

> **1:26** And ELOHIM said, "Let <u>us</u> make soil-creature in <u>our</u> image, according to <u>our</u> likeness, and let them govern in the fish of the sea, and with the flyer of the skies, and in the animals, and in all the land, and in every moving thing that moves about upon the land."

> **3:22** And YHVH ELOHIM said, "Look!—the soil-creature has become like one from <u>us</u>,[78] to know good and bad; and now, lest he send forth his hand and take also from the tree of life, and eat, and live for an age . . . !"

The confusion, in part, arises because monotheism is a very recent term coined by British philosopher Henry More (1614-1687 CE). Modern people tend to assume the concept of monotheism has been around for thousands of years, when that may not be the case.

Due to the plural pronouns in Genesis 1-3, biblical scholars largely agree that pantheism or henotheism were the likely

---

[78] Or "from him," pronoun can mean "us" or "him" here.

viewpoints depicted therein. Most ancient cultures were either pantheistic or henotheistic. My argument here is not that we should believe in one god or many gods, but instead to focus without bias on what the text actually contains, which in this case, does not appear to be monotheism.

Strangely, throughout the text, God is referred to with the pronoun "He," which is confusing because God is also described as plural, as we saw in the quotes above. To make sense of the pronoun confusion, we should be mindful that Hebrew is a grammatically gendered language, like Latin, which means all nouns are assigned a gender. Due to Hebrew's linguistic structure, even the word "God" must be given a gendered pronoun. Clearly gender is irrelevant to the Infinite, so it is helpful to erase any sense of gender from our minds when it comes to the Infinite.

The creation mythology in Genesis is unusual in still another important and obvious way: it seems to contain two distinct and largely incompatible creation stories. Although biblical scholars overwhelmingly agree that two distinct creation stories appear in Genesis, the clergy, almost without exception, reject the idea. That said, the observation of two incompatible creation myths within Genesis is nothing new. About 2,000 years ago, Philo Judaeus of Alexandria, a Jewish philosopher, commented on the contradictions of Genesis 1 and 2. He did not see the contradictions as a problem, though, for he considered the stories allegorical in nature rather than historical accounts of creation.

The paradigmatic shift from historical representation to allegory is not a step that the majority of modern religious elders have been willing to take. The religious insistence that the stories are accurate historical accounts causes those leaders to close their hearts and minds to other possibilities. One cannot discover the code with such a closed perspective. Let us be careful not to close our hearts and minds in this way.

To see the two stories, turn to *The Book of Genesis* located at the end of this book and notice the first creation story begins at Genesis 1 and continues to Genesis 2:3. The second creation story goes from Genesis 2:4 to Genesis 2:9. The inconsistencies and contradictions between the two stories are too numerous to warrant full inclusion here. Some are quite easy to see, while others require a trained eye and a little sleuthing to notice. Here, I will point out some of the major issues and leave the rest to biblical scholars.

Probably the most obvious inconsistency can be seen in the naming of God, which differs between the two stories. If you pay attention to the text, you will notice that in the first creation story, the creator is exclusively called ELOHIM; in the second creation story, the creator, with very few exceptions, is called YHVH ELOHIM. Most modern English Bibles translate YHVH into "LORD" and ELOHIM into "GOD," so in a modern English Bible, you would see the creator written as "God" or "GOD" in Genesis 1-2:3 and generally "LORD GOD" or "Lord God" from Genesis 2:4 onward.

Anthropological research reveals that there were two primary ancestral Jewish tribes that merged over time: the Northern tribes of Judah, who worshipped YHVH (Yahveh), and the Southern tribes, the Israelites, who lived in the area today known as Israel, Palestine, and Lebanon. We find record of the Israelites' worship in the book of Judges 10:6, where it is written that the Israelites "served the Baals and the Ashtoreths, and the gods of Aram, the gods of Sidon, the gods of Moab, the gods of the Ammonites and the gods of the Philistines."

Apparently, these were the traditional gods that ancient Israelites collectively called ELOHIM. El was a generalized term for "deity" and was used to describe any of the gods worshipped in the area. ELOHIM is the plural of El and alludes to henotheism. Although ELOHIM is commonly translated as a singular God in modern Judaism, that was not the case before the tribes unified. If we look at the names of the angels, we can see that they end in "el"—Michael, Raphael, Gabriel, and Uriel.

Many scholars speculate that the amalgamation of gods that made up ELOHIM inspired the subsequent Jewish idea of God and his angels, as well as the Greek pantheon, headed by Zeus. In any case, prior to the unification of the tribes, ELOHIM represented many gods.

Biblical scholars argue that to facilitate harmony between merging tribes, homogenizing their creation myths was required. Genesis 1-3 seems to verify the homogenization. Let's explore that idea a bit further.

It appears that YHVH (thought to have been pronounced "Yahveh" or "Yehovah") believers, referred to by biblical scholars as "Yahvehists" came to think of YHVH as the one true creator of all the cosmos. As such, following all other gods was prohibited. Believers of ELOHIM were brought into the religion of YHVH through merging the creation stories and names of their deities, YHVH and ELOHIM. This merger can be seen in Genesis 2, where the creator's name is YHVH ELOHIM.

During the Second Temple period, it was considered taboo to utter the name "Yahveh", which is why it is Jewish practice to substitute the tetragrammaton (YHVH) with the word "Adonai" meaning "Lord."

More evidence of the disparate origins of the two creation stories can be seen in their different focal points. The first story depicts cosmic creation with no particular focus on humans. It does not include the creation of humans until day six, the final day of creation.

The second story, which is not ordered by days as is the first story, is focused first and foremost on the creation of Adam and Eve. Only after the creation of the first human does the creator create other things such as plants, animals, and the garden named "Eden," in which the man was to live and caretake. The description of the second creation story begins at Genesis 2:4:

> **4 These** *are* **the bringings-forth of the skies and the land**[31] in their being created. In *the* day of the making[32] of YHVH[33] ELOHIM, land and skies, **5** and no shrub of the field was before *that* on the land, and no plant of the field had before *that* sprouted—for YHVH ELOHIM had not made rain[c] on the land, and there *was* no soil-creature to service the soil; **6** and a flow would go up from the land, and it made drink[c] all the face[p] of the soil—**7** and YHVH ELOHIM shaped the soil-creature—dust from the soil, and he blew into his two nostrils breath of life[p]; and the soil-creature became a living life-breather. **8** And YHVH ELOHIM planted a garden in Eden, at the east; and there he placed the soil-creature whom he shaped. We can see in the first story that the creator made everything before he made humans, but in the second account, he created man before he created plants, animals, and Eden.

---

[31] Genesis has ten divisions, each beginning with the phrase "These *are* the bringings-forth of . . ." and these are indicated in this translation by **bold type**.

[32] Lit "doing."

[33] Name of the God of Israel יהוה (Tetragrammaton), traditionally Yahveh, or Yehovah; translated LORD in most English versions but here left as four letters without vowels.

The stories also demonstrate a great difference in the way that human beings were created. In Genesis 1, God speaks them into being as follows:

> **26** And ELOHIM said, "Let us make soil-creature[23] in our image, according to our likeness, and let them govern in the fish of the sea, and with the flyer of the skies, and in the animals[s], and in all the land, and in every moving thing that moves about upon the land." **27** And ELOHIM created the soil-creature in his image: in the image of ELOHIM he created him, a male and a female he created them. **28** And ELOHIM blessed them and ELOHIM said to them, "Bear fruit and be abundant and fill the land; and subdue, and govern in the fish of the sea, and in the flyer of the skies, and in every living thing that moves about upon the land." **29** And ELOHIM said, "Look!—I have given to you[p] every plant seeding seed that *is* upon the face[p] of all the land, and every tree[d], in which *there is* fruit of a tree, seeding seed; to you[p] it will be for an eatable *thing*. **30** And to every living thing of the land, and to every flyer of the skies, and to every moving about thing on the land, that in it *is* living life-breath—every green plant *is* for an eatable *thing*." And it was thus.

As we can see in Genesis 1, human beings are spoken into being. Males and females are created simultaneously. In the second story, the creator molds man from soil and breathes the breath of life into

---

[23] Heb *'adam*, from *'adamah*, "soil," or "red soil."

him. Man is made first, after which woman is made from flesh taken from the side of the man, as is shown below:

> **21** And YHVH ELOHIM made a deep sleep fall[c] upon the soil-creature, and he slept; and he took one from his sides, and he closed flesh under it. **22** And YHVH ELOHIM built the side that he took from the soil-creature into a woman, and he made her come[c] toward the soil-creature. **23** And the soil-creature said, "This one this time—bone of my bones, and flesh of my flesh! To this one will be called "woman," because from a man this one was taken."

Because the creation stories focus on the creator, how the stories present the Infinite is probably the most important distinction. In the first story, the Infinite is portrayed as being outside of or prior to existence. The Infinite speaks things into existence from nothing. In the second story, by contrast, the Infinite is depicted as a boots-on-the ground character who interacts with the humans in the garden as if he were an embodied being.

These two distinct creation stories, although clearly not of the same origin, appear to have been edited together in such a way as to allow for the unification of the two tribes. What I find especially interesting is the fact that the code could not exist without the splicing and editing of these two stories. I have no way of determining with certainty whether the code was intentional and not a cosmic "happenstance," but the code clearly depends upon the stories being connected as they are. And the way that the code is presented to us in Genesis is just as it would have been presented to Jesus 2,000 years ago because extant texts stretch back roughly to the time of Jesus.

The oddities of the Genesis creation stories are indeed quite remarkable. Let's keep them in mind as we move forward, being careful to soften our beliefs and set aside any biases we might have toward the nature of the Infinite, the relationship between the Infinite and humanity, and the meaning of sin and the fall.

Chapter 8

The Mirror of Genesis

We have discussed the dangers of religion being replaced by ideology, a trend that seems to escalate with the precipitous demise of religion, and little else to provide a higher aim and lend a sense of meaning to life. Now we should turn our attention to the danger of blind belief in religious stories.

Many religious believers hold that Genesis is the historical account of creation. They do not accept the idea that the creation stories are metaphorical or open to interpretation. To maintain that stance, they reject out of hand the idea that there are two distinct, largely incompatible stories within Genesis. Literalists not only deny the poetic qualities of Genesis but also the massive amount of textual scholarship showing that these indeed are different texts edited together.

To get a sense for the literalist perspective, you might do an Internet search for "Catholic Answers what is the JEPD Theory?"

If you believe your good standing with God depends upon seeing The Holy Bible as factual and infallible, then, reasonably, you would not entertain any other perspective. Unfortunately, such barriers blind the mind to possible faults, inconsistencies, and hypocrisies in the text. Such faults include the endorsement of many ideas that our current society would consider abhorrent, such as slavery and genocide.

I've yet to meet a believer, including the most extreme of fundamentalists, who endorsed slavery or genocide. Why aren't modern Jews and Christians endorsing slavery? Nowhere in these texts is slavery described as wrong. On the contrary, there are many passages that praise God for the enslavement of enemies. The fact is that we are picking and choosing what to believe. Since we are already deciding which pieces of the text are applicable to our lives, we would be wise to admit this openly, so as not to deceive ourselves or others.

The Bible is a book of its time. It endorses behaviors that we no longer accept. But that is not all it is. The Holy Bible contains profoundly deep wisdom, such as *the principle* found in Genesis 1-3. We as human beings have the responsibility to notice what the text actually says and then to use our discernment about the text, according to our values. To do otherwise is to cede our responsibility to someone else, an author or authors from thousands of years ago in a society with norms and values that may not be compatible with ours or those of our society.

To an attentive, non-biased reader, the inconsistencies between Genesis 1 and 2 are readily apparent, as is the hypocritical way in which God is portrayed in Genesis 3. The Holy Bible says an all-knowing, all-powerful God created all of the elements and temptations that would surely result in humans falling into suffering. Viewed from that perspective, Genesis 2-3 seems to be the rough equivalent of a parent who leaves a bunch of uncovered wall sockets in the baby's room, warns the baby, and then punishes it for getting shocked.

Before receiving the code through mystical experience, I felt unable to see much value in the text because I was blinded by my sensitivities to the many hypocrisies and atrocities committed in the name of or at the command of God in other biblical stories. But after seeing the code, my eyes and heart were opened to the book.

Somehow, through or despite the enslavement of the Jews in Egypt, the blending of cultures, the splicing and editing, and the layers of cultural and mythological teachings, the code is there. How it could have survived all of that is a great mystery to me, especially considering the remarkable mirrorlike quality of Genesis 1-3.

It seems to me that Genesis 1-3 reflects the reader's judgments and biases. On the surface, the stories are culturally based, much like creation stories found around the world, but at a deeper level, the level of *principle*, the message of Genesis 1-3 is universal. The hidden teaching applies to and can benefit any human being who is open to it, regardless of country, ethnicity, culture, class, or gender.

Because of the biased minds of prophets, priests, and scribes who, it seems, did not have the eyes to see, almost all subsequent scripture emphasizes superficial or overt aspects in Genesis, such as the cultural rules, the supernatural story, and the judgment of humanity. For thousands of years the shallow view of these stories has fueled blame, shame, guilt, arrogance, resentment, and false humility.

Genesis 1-3, superficially interpreted, provides a poor spiritual foundation, which has led to so much misunderstanding and disharmony as false teachings have spread worldwide through organized religious movements. For example, one of the primary ideas that has spread as a result of misinterpreting Genesis is the justification for the objectification of nature. The verses where misinterpretation has led to this worldwide trend are well represented by most modern interpretations of Genesis 1:26-28. Let's look to the New International Version as an example:

> 26 Then God said, "Let us make mankind in our image, in our likeness, so that they may rule over the fish in the sea and the birds in the sky, over the livestock and all the wild animals, and over all the creatures that move along the ground." 27 So God created mankind in his own image, in the image of God he created them; male and female he created them. 28 God blessed them and said to them, "Be fruitful and increase in number; fill the earth and subdue it. Rule over the fish in the sea and the birds in the sky and over every living creature that moves on the ground."

Many societies justify ecologically unsound actions with reference to this passage's focus on humanity's domination over nature. This objectifying state of mind misses the point of Genesis, which is meant to depict harmony with all of life. The selfish state of mind, justified by a poor understanding of Genesis, causes unnecessary disharmony in our lives and the world.

Much like looking into a mirror, when we read Genesis, we tend to see what we bring with us. In fact, those first three chapters can be read in two very different ways. How we interpret them has a profoundly different impact on our lives and social development. We will discuss this in depth later. For now, let's take a look at these same passages through Dr. Tabor's interpretation.

26 And ELOHIM said, "Let us make soil-creature[23] in our image, according to our likeness, and let them govern in[24] the fish of the sea, and with the flyer of the skies, and in the animals[s], and in all the land,[25] and in every moving thing that moves about upon the land." **27** And ELOHIM created the soil-creature in his image: in the image of ELOHIM he created him, a male and a female he created them. **28** And ELOHIM blessed them and ELOHIM said to them, "Bear fruit and be abundant and fill the land; and subdue, and govern in the fish of the sea, and in the flyer of the skies, and in every living thing that moves about upon the land."

Dr. Tabor's translation stresses governance and is much more aligned with God's stated purpose for creating Adam and Eve, as can be seen in Genesis 2:15:

15 And YHVH ELOHIM took the soil-creature and made him rest[c] in the garden of Eden, to service it and to guard it.

To subdue, service, guard, and govern. Those directives are perfectly aligned with gardening, the process of taking what would otherwise be overly chaotic and creating a harmonious order for the purpose of the health of the land and its inhabitants. Fundamentally, Genesis directs human beings to commune with nature through proper leadership and proper harvesting. This is also the general sentiment of indigenous peoples worldwide. And

---

[23] Heb *'adam*, from *'adamah*, "soil," or "red soil."
[24] I.e., in regard to, here and v. 28.
[25] Syriac "over all the animals of the land."

why wouldn't that be the case? After all, the ancient Hebrews were tribes much like any other, living at one with the earth.

Sometime relatively recently in the span of human existence, many human societies lost their sense of relationship with the earth and with the Infinite. As a result, many of us have been living like parasites on the planet. That parasitic way of living can never truly satisfy, for it is not in alignment with our nature.

We've regarded the planet as existing to be used by us for our own narrow purposes for too long. No longer can we turn a blind eye to our mistakes, for nature is beginning to show us the consequences of objectification. The idea that the earth and its flora, fauna, minerals, et cetera, are merely resources to use and discard is starting to hurt us now. The pain may serve to wake us from the dream of separation.

In fact, we've become so used to objectification that we do it to ourselves without even realizing it. In our own minds, we have become little more than commodities. If you don't yet see that, when you recognize the code and how it works in your life, you may no longer be able to avoid seeing it.

If humanity were to heed the covert teaching of Genesis, *the principle*, then individuals and societies might be far less enamored with blame, shame, guilt, arrogance, resentment and false humility. As a result, we could more easily find balance with each other and our environment and thereby live more inspired, meaningful lives in communion with *all-that-is*.

The common atheistic idea that The Holy Bible is merely an artifact of an ignorant people starts to fall short when we see the consistency of the code. Based on the embedded *principle*, which demonstrates the real cause of psychological and spiritual suffering, as well as the pathway to harmony, I'm not sure we should be so quick to dismiss the text.

As to how *the principle* got there, I remain on the fence. It seems to me that either *the principle* was intentionally edited in, possibly to protect a secret, or it got there through the unwitting genius that sometimes shines through creative people. To me, either way is mind-boggling and equally magnificent.

I would like to think that the code was edited into the text as a way of preserving for posterity a secret that needed protecting from people that would be hostile to the teachings at the time. We can relate this idea to Jesus' explanation that he intentionally hides the truth from the masses. Why would he do this, one must wonder? Maybe Jesus was trying to avoid persecution. Remember: Jesus was crucified for blasphemy. Why should we assume the priestly class of earlier times was any more tolerant? Maybe you will have a different hypothesis after seeing the code. Let's get to it!

Part 3

The Code

In Part 2, we familiarized ourselves with creation mythology commonalities, which provided us with a comparative lens through which we could view Genesis 1-3. We then learned of the oddities of Genesis born from splicing two separate mythologies together. Finally, we learned of the traps of blind belief in religion and ideology. What we have learned has helped prepare our eyes to see the code.

In Part 3, which comprises four chapters, we explore the three perspectives of Genesis that make up the code.

Chapter 9 explores the perspective of the disembodied Infinite, called ELOHIM in Genesis 1. This chapter demonstrates the foundational attitude of harmony.

Chapter 10 introduces the perspective of the embodied Infinite, called YHVH ELOHIM, as depicted in Genesis 2. This chapter demonstrates a healthy foundational psychology for human beings.

Chapter 11 focuses on Genesis 3 and the perspective of the disharmony that naturally results when the embodied Infinite forgets its infinite nature and becomes self-absorbed in its form-based identity.

Finally, Chapter 12 reveals the layers of the code and shows how *the principle* maps onto the human experience through evolution and the childhood developmental process, as well as through the revelatory experiences of prayer and meditation.

By any measure, The Holy Bible has been read by more people than all other books. Despite the flaws discussed above, billions of people worldwide feel immense spiritual value resides in this text. Our conscious minds may not yet be able to fully articulate the precise nature of the text's offering, but once you have perceived and incorporated *the principle* into your life, you will be far more able to do so.

Genesis has been read by billions of people over the ages. Anyone who has read Genesis 1-3 has seen the code, but in all that time, it seems, the code has gone unperceived. No longer! Once you *see* it, you won't be able to *unsee* it.

The code is simple, elegant, and practical. Once you put the code into practice through your daily life, it will begin to unravel the layers of inner disharmony and confusion. You will never look at yourself or life in quite the same way. Your relationship with everything will change.

Chapter 9

The Infinite God

The Disembodied Infinite

As we saw in Chapter 7, two creation stories of the tribes of Judah and the Israelites have been spliced together in Genesis 1-3. Within the spliced mythologies we may observe three primary perspectives: the disembodied Infinite, the embodied Infinite, and the self-absorbed Infinite. These three disparate perspectives provide the foundation of the code.

The first perspective is found in Genesis 1, as the Infinite "speaks" the Universe into existence. Please read the full text of Genesis 1 below and note the <u>underlined text</u>, which represents the yellow highlighting, relevant to this chapter, that I saw as the code when it was presented to me through a visionary state. Once we have viewed the underlined text within the context of the chapter, we will break down the meaning of those sentences to establish a foundational understanding of *the principle*.

(Bere'sheet)

Chapter **1:1** At *the* first[f2] of ELOHIM[3] creating the skies and the land—**2** and the land was desolation and emptiness; and darkness *was* over *the* face[p] of *the* deep, and the spirit of ELOHIM was hovering over the face[p] of the waters— **3** and ELOHIM said, "Let there be light"; and it was light. **4** <u>And ELOHIM saw the light, that *it was* good</u>; and ELOHIM separated between the light and between the darkness. **5** And ELOHIM called to the light "day," and to the darkness he called "night." And it was evening and it was morning—day one.

6 And ELOHIM said, "Let there be an expanse in the middle of the waters, and let there be a separating between waters to waters." **7** And ELOHIM made the expanse, and he separated between the waters that *were* from under the expanse, and between the waters that *were* from upon the expanse. And it was thus. **8** And ELOHIM called to the expanse "skies." And it was evening and it was morning, a second day. **9** And ELOHIM said, "Let the waters under the skies be gathered toward one place, and let the dry *land.* be seen." And it was thus. **10** And ELOHIM called to the dry *land* "land," and to the collection of the waters he called "seas." <u>And ELOHIM saw that *it was* good.</u> **11** And ELOHIM said, "Let the land sprout[c] *the* sprout, a plant seeding seed, a fruit tree making fruit, according to its type,

---

[2] Lit "At *the* head of," Heb *Bere'sheet* in this grammatical construction is a temporal phrase meaning, "When at first . . .," see Jer 26:1 where the same form occurs. It presents the "state of things" when the creative activity begins.

[3] ELOHIM is a plural noun, but often functions as a collective singular, taking a singular verb. It is related to the Hebrew terms: *'eloah* and *'el,* meaning God, god, power, or mighty one, and can refer to judges and leaders, heavenly beings, the gods of the nations, or the one God of Israel.

its seed, within it, upon the land." And it was thus. **12** And the land made *the* sprout go out^c, a plant seeding seed according to its type, and a tree making fruit, its seed, within it, according to its type. <u>And ELOHIM saw that *it was* good.</u> **13** And it was evening and it was morning, a third day.

14 And ELOHIM said, "Let there be lights in the expanse of the skies, to separate between the day and between the night; and they will be for signs, and for appointed times, and for days and years, **15** and they will be for lights in the expanse of the skies, to make light^c upon the land." And it was thus. **16** And ELOHIM made the two large lights—the large light for rule of the day, and the small light for rule of the night—and the stars. **17** And ELOHIM gave them in the expanse of the skies, to make light^c upon the land, **18** and to rule in the day and in the night, and to separate between the light and between the darkness. <u>And ELOHIM saw that *it was* good.</u> **19** And it was evening and it was morning, a fourth day.

20 And ELOHIM said, "Let the waters swarm a swarm of living life-breathers^s, and let *the* flyer fly upon the land, upon the face^p of the expanse of the skies." **21** And ELOHIM created the large *water*-beasts, and every living^d life-breather that moves about, *with* which the waters swarm, according to their type, and every winged flyer, according to its type. <u>And ELOHIM saw that *it was* good.</u> **22** And ELOHIM blessed them saying, "Bear fruit and be abundant and fill the waters in the seas, and let the flyer be abundant in the land." **23** And it was evening and it was morning, a fifth day.

24 And ELOHIM said, "Let the land make a living life-breather go out^c according to its type: animal, and moving thing, and living thing of land according to its type." And it was thus. **25** And ELOHIM made the living thing of the land, according to its type, and the animal according to its type, and every moving thing of the soil according to its type. And ELOHIM saw that *it was* good. **26** And ELOHIM said, "Let us make soil-creature in our image, according to our likeness, and let them govern in the fish of the sea, and with the flyer of the skies, and in the animals^s, and in all the land, and in every moving thing that moves about upon the land." **27** And ELOHIM created the soil-creature in his image: in the image of ELOHIM he created him, a male and a female he created them. **28** And ELOHIM blessed them and ELOHIM said to them, "Bear fruit and be abundant and fill the land; and subdue, and govern in the fish of the sea, and in the flyer of the skies, and in every living thing that moves about upon the land." **29** And ELOHIM said, "Look!—I have given to you^p every plant seeding seed that *is* upon the face^p of all the land, and every tree^d, in which *there is* fruit of a tree, seeding seed; to you^p it will be for an eatable *thing*. **30** And to every living thing of the land, and to every flyer of the skies, and to every moving about thing on the land, that in it *is* living life-breath—every green plant *is* for an eatable *thing*." And it was thus. **31** And ELOHIM saw all that he had made, and look!—*it was* exceedingly good. And it was evening and it was morning, the sixth day.

The code as I was shown it was entirely about attitude and perspective, not about culture, societal laws, the order of created things and beings, or how many days it took to create the earth. With attention to attitude and perspective, let us review the code as highlighted in mystical experience.

Looking at the underlined text, we see that it is a repeated and sometimes slightly varied expression of "And ELOHIM saw that *it was* good." You'll note that nowhere in Genesis 1 is there anything but praise for the good of creation.

The perfect consistency of attitude reflects the nature of the Infinite; thus, we are wise to pay attention. The question is what does the Infinite mean by *good*?

To find the definition of *good*, first consider how human beings define it: a reflection of whatever is in alignment with our values, aims, and or comforts, what is pleasant. Merriam-Webster defines good as follows:

1 : the pleasant things that happen to people
2 : things that are morally proper or correct

From these definitions we can see that *good* as it is defined by humans is highly subjective. We define good in opposition to what we assume is bad. Is the *good* of the Infinite similarly subjective and comparative? Is it moral in nature?

From the perspective of the Infinite there is no other, which means that the Infinite does not see the Universe as something other than itself, as is hinted at in Genesis 1. Therefore, we may take this to mean that *good* in this case is whatever is in alignment with the Infinite, which is to say whatever reflects itself. The Infinite *good* is that which is synonymous with the Infinite. With the Infinite definition of *good* in mind, the sentence "And ELOHIM saw that it was good" means "And ELOHIM saw that it was ELOHIM," or "And God saw that it was God."

ELOHIM's praise is repeated 7 times in Genesis 1, which stresses just how fundamental the perspective of oneness and praise is.

Before we dig deeper into the underlined sentences, notice also the italicized word, *was*. The Tabor Translation Reader's Guide explains the meaning of italics thusly: "*Italic* Type indicates words **not** in the Hebrew but supplied for smoother English style."

In the sentence "And ELOHIM saw that *it was* good," the choice, *was*, conjures the idea that ELOHIM's opinion of creation could change, when that cannot be the case, for the Infinite does not see anything other than itself.

To avoid this meaning trap and to complete the sentence as readers rightly expect, it would be better to use the present verb *is* instead of *was*. This word choice captures the ever-present perspective of the Infinite, "There is no other." *No other* is *the principle*, indicated by Genesis 1.

I hope readers will refresh the text in their minds, remembering that creation is an ever-present witnessing and praising in the moment; a revelation that has always been and will always be—the Witness. To help us focus more clearly on that perspective, below I have revised all sentences of praise so that they reflect the present tense. To begin to get a sense of the Infinite perspective as you read, you will need to relax and deeply feel your entire body.

Below I list each instance of praise found in Genesis 1, but in the present tense and as a revelation of potential instead of definitive creation. To aid us in this endeavor, I've removed gendered language for God, which is an unhelpful Hebrew grammatical rule that misleads us about the nature of the Infinite. The disembodied Infinite is not specifically male or female.

Before each praise, I include the target of the praise. Please take a moment to visualize the target of each praise and then read aloud the praise while feeling the vibrations of the words as they are uttered toward the intended target.

1. Light — "And God sees the light, that *it is* God"
2. Land and seas — "And God sees that *it is* God"
3. Plants and trees — "And God sees that *it is* God"
4. Sun, moon, stars — "And God sees that *it is* God"
5. Water creatures and flyers — "And God sees that *it is* God"
6. Land creatures— "And God sees that *it is* God"
7. All that is — "And God sees all that is, and look!—*it is* exceedingly God."

The mind cannot fully understand the seamless nature of the Infinite because the default setting of the mind is to categorize things for a functional understanding. The Infinite can't be understood, but it *can* be felt. For the best effect, leave off intellectualizing for now; just visualize and feel your body as you speak the words with intention. The words without the visualization and feeling will never get us there.

As we can see from the text, the Infinite praises everything. Regarding human beings, ELOHIM said, "Let us make soil-creature in our image, according to our likeness".

According to Genesis 1, you are the image and likeness of God. With that in mind, look in the mirror, and while feeling your entire body, repeat and feel, "And God sees that I am God."

Practice and a little light stretching to release tension will help resolve the unhelpful judgment and feelings of separation held within the subconscious mind.

Now, look around you. To everyone and everything you see, repeat with feeling, "And God sees that it is completely, seamlessly God."

Note: The last quoted sentence as well as the numbered sentences are my own formulations based on the principle of Genesis 1.

Chapter 10

God Incarnate
The Embodied Infinite

Genesis 2 begins with the splice used to merge two separate creation stories. You might recall that we introduced the evidence of this merger in Chapter 7. The splice runs from Genesis 2:1 to 2:3. To verify that Genesis 2.4 is the start of the story as intended in the original text, you will notice through all 53 chapters of Genesis there are special demarcations at the start of stories, all of which use the same phrase, "These are the bringings-forth of". The content germane to this chapter does not begin until Genesis 2:4, where the second creator mythology begins. You can see the splice here:

Chapter **2:1** And the skies and the land and all their company were finished. **2** And ELOHIM finished on the seventh day his work that he did, and he ceased on the seventh day from all his work that he did. **3** And ELOHIM blessed the seventh day, and he set it apart, because on it he ceased from all his work that ELOHIM created to do.

4 These *are* the bringings-forth of the skies and the land in their being created.

The Infinite does not rest, for it does not tire. It continually, joyously, and effortlessly brings forth its image in praise. Rest is for the embodied Infinite, not the disembodied Infinite. Rest is necessary to maintain the health of the body, but the teaching of rest is not the code. This splice brings us to the focus of this chapter, Genesis 2.

Genesis 2 represents the perspective of the "children of God," which is to say the Infinite as expressed through the experience of human beings. Although differences in perspective exist between the embodied expression of the Infinite and the disembodied Infinite, we want to keep alert for an important through-line. That through-line is the code. Please see the underlined text in Genesis 2 for the code.

4 These *are* the bringings-forth of the skies and the land[31] in their being created. In *the* day of the making of YHVH[33] ELOHIM, land and skies, **5** and no shrub of the field was before *that* on the land, and no plant of the field had before *that* sprouted—for YHVH ELOHIM had not made rain[c] on the land, <u>and there *was* no soil-creature to service the soil</u>;

---

[31] Genesis has ten divisions, each beginning with the phrase "These *are* the bringings-forth of . . ." and these are indicated in this translation by **bold type**.

[33] Name of the God of Israel יהוה (Tetragrammaton), traditionally Yahveh, or Yehovah; translated LORD in most English versions but here left as four letters without vowels.

6 and a flow would go up from the land, and it made drink^c all the face^p of the soil—**7** <u>and YHVH ELOHIM shaped the</u> <u>soil-creature—dust from the soil, and he blew into his two</u> <u>nostrils breath of life^p; and the soil-creature became a living</u> <u>life-breather.</u> **8** And YHVH ELOHIM planted a garden in Eden,[38] at the east; and there he placed the soil-creature whom he shaped. **9** <u>And YHVH ELOHIM made sprout^c</u> <u>from the soil every tree desired for sight and good for an</u> <u>eatable *thing*; and the tree of life^p in the middle of the</u> <u>garden, and the tree of the knowledge of good and bad.</u> **10** And a river goes out from Eden to make drink^c the garden, and from there it is separated and it becomes four heads. **11** The name of the one *is* Pishon; it goes around all the land of the Havilah, where there *is* gold^d, **12** and the gold of that land *is* good; there *are* bdellium and the onyx stone. **13** And the name of the second river *is* Gihon; it goes around all the land of Cush. **14** And the name of the third river *is* Hiddekel; it *is* the one walking east of Assyria. And the fourth river—it *is* Euphrates. **15** And YHVH ELOHIM took the soil-creature and made him rest^c in the garden of Eden, to service it and to guard it. **16** And YHVH ELOHIM *laid* charge upon the soil-creature, saying, "From every tree of the garden, eating—you will *surely* eat![44] **17** <u>And from</u> <u>the tree of the knowledge of good and bad, you will not eat</u> <u>from it; for on *the* day you eat from it, dying—you will</u> <u>*surely* die!"</u>[45] **18** And YHVH ELOHIM said, "<u>Not good—</u> <u>the soil-creature being by himself,</u> I will make for him a

---

[38] Name of a place or region, meaning "pleasure" or "bliss."

[44] Double use of the verb indicates emphasis.

[45] Double use of the verb indicates emphasis.

help, as his *one* before." **19** And YHVH ELOHIM shaped from the soil every living thing of the field, and every flyer of the skies, and he made come^c toward the soil-creature to see what he would call to it; and whatever the soil-creature would call to it—*each* living life-breather—that *was* its name. **20** And the soil-creature called names to every animal, and to the flyer of the skies, and to every living thing of the field; and to *Soil-creature* he did not find a help, as his *one* before. **21** And YHVH ELOHIM made a deep sleep fall^c upon the soil-creature, and he slept; and he took one from his sides, and he closed flesh under it. **22** And YHVH ELOHIM built the side that he took from the soil-creature into a woman, and he made her come^c toward the soil-creature. **23** And the soil-creature said, "This one this time—bone of my bones, and flesh of my flesh! To this one will be called "woman," because from a man this one was taken." **24** Therefore a man will leave his father and his mother, and join with his woman, and they become one flesh. **25** <u>And the *two* of them were nude,—the soil-creature and his woman—and they were not ashamed.</u>

Having read through the entire passage, let us review and reflect. The first underlined sentence is as follows:

there *was* no soil-creature to service the soil

This sentence identifies humanity's purpose. We can see that this very same mandate was expressed in Genesis 1:

let them govern in the fish of the sea, and with the flyer of
the skies, and in the animals, and in all the land, and in
every moving thing that moves about upon the land.

Just after the Infinite creates humans in Genesis 1, they repeat the
human mandate, which is to govern every living thing. The
mandate is not to take, but to caretake, which you can clearly see
in the passage below:

subdue, and govern in the fish of the sea, and in the flyer
of the skies, and in every living thing that moves about
upon the land.

Now let's look at how the soil-creature, known as Adam, was
created in Genesis 2 to see what of value might be there.

YHVH ELOHIM shaped the soil-creature—dust from the
soil, and he blew into his two nostrils breath of life; and the
soil-creature became a living life-breather.

Look at your body, at its naturalness. Can you find anything of it
that is not earth? We are soil and air through and through. And the
atoms that make up our bodies and the earth are completely born
of the stars. The stars, like all things, represent the body of the
Infinite. Everything we see, hear, smell, taste, touch, feel, or think
is one seamless revelation of the Infinite. Remember, in Genesis 1,
ELOHIM "created the soil-creature in his image: in the image of
ELOHIM he created him, a male and a female he created them."

We humans are the image and likeness of the Infinite because
the soil is the image and likeness of the Infinite, as is the air we
breathe, the planet, the solar system, the galaxy, and the entire

Universe. All of it, all of you, is the body of the Infinite. There is nothing that you can point to or think of, no matter how seemingly far from the Infinite you judge it to be, that is not the Witness that we explored in Chapter 3.

You might consider those people who maliciously caused the massacre and starvation of tens or hundreds of millions of people, like Joseph Stalin, Adolf Hitler or Mao Zedong, and then feel doubt about all being the Infinite, all being good according to its perspective. How could those people possibly represent the Infinite? This question directly relates to a warning to Adam found in Genesis 2, not to eat of the tree of the knowledge of good and bad.

> And from the tree of the knowledge of good and bad, you will not eat from it; for on *the* day you eat from it, dying— you will *surely* die!

What is this warning about, you might wonder? What is the tree of the knowledge of good and bad? Disharmony and the tree of the knowledge of good and bad are related topics found in Genesis 3, which we will discuss in the next chapter. For now, let's continue with Genesis 2.

In the very next sentence of Genesis 2, we can see the first reference to something being *not good*.

> And YHVH ELOHIM said, "Not good—the soil-creature being by himself, I will make for him a help, as his *one* before."

Isn't *not good* the same thing as *bad*? In this case, not good simply means incomplete. Essentially, the Infinite is saying more needs to be done to reflect the balanced nature of the Infinite. *Not good*, in this case, does not mean *bad* or *evil*. I have underlined it so that the *not good* here will not throw you off the track of our discussion.

The fact that the story reverses the roles of men and women with regard to creation—Eve being created from Adam—feels more like a cultural teaching that is intended to reinforce a patriarchal society. This aspect of the story does not reflect the code.

This brings us to the last of the code found in Genesis 2:

> And the *two* of them were nude—the soil-creature and his woman—and they were not ashamed.

If you've ever been around young children, they, like Adam and Eve, can walk around naked without an ounce of self-consciousness. If you look back on your life, can you recall when you lost that innocent state? How old were you?

You see, Adam and Eve, here, are at the stage of innocence like that of young children. They do not have a self-conscious voice in their heads telling them how other people will think of them. They do not have an inner voice that measures their self-worth or the worth of others. The innocent mind described in Genesis 2 is a core element of the code.

The key point to remember from this chapter is the pure act of caretaking that is the mandate of the embodied Infinite—Adam and Eve. So long as they are in the flow of caretaking, they clearly feel the harmony of the Infinite in their lives.

Think about your life. Is there anything that you do or did that feels like true caretaking? It would be an act of service, done lovingly, that gains you nothing at the level of ego. What we are indicating is a communion where everyone is served, including you, without a sense of self-absorption or codependency regarding the service. Whatever it is that you do that fits this definition is an activity that is in alignment with your truest nature, the Infinite within you. Whatever that activity is benefits everyone and everything in some way. You might allow yourself to do more of that.

Artistic, creative, and inspiring activities are best included in the caretaking category, for they nourish the soul. They are caretaking, so long as you partake in them innocently, joyfully, with all of your being, and share them with an open heart, unconcerned about how you might be judged. Becoming well-known or accepting money for the products of these nourishing activities is fine so long as reputation and wealth are not the primary motivating forces.

Chapter 11

The Serpent
The Self-Absorbed Infinite

The serpent of Eden has been considered the enemy of God, the spanner in the works, for thousands of years. Although it is never directly stated in Genesis 1-3 or anywhere else in the Hebrew Bible, the serpent is assumed to be the essence of evil—Satan. How did Satan become associated with the serpent of Eden?

There are no references to Satan as a personal name in the original Hebrew; instead, Satan is written as "*the satan*." However, modern English translations falsely represent the term as a personal name. To correct the issue, I will stick to the original presentation, *the satan*, in my commentary.

The term *the satan* simply means "accuser," "adversary," or "to oppose." The term can be applied to any adversary, accuser, or opposition, including human beings, but is also associated with angelic forces said to be "sent" by God.

The first such reference in the Hebrew Bible is found in Numbers 22:22. There *the satan* is used as a verb meaning to oppose:

> But GOD was very angry when he went, and the angel of the LORD stood in the road to oppose him (to satan, him). Balaam was riding on his donkey, and his two servants were with him.

Anyone standing on the road aiming to oppose Balaam would have been described as *the satan*, the opposition. No implication of evil is implied by this use of the term *satan*. Whatever gets in the way of your aim could be described as *the satan* in ancient Hebrew.

Another reference to *the satan* occurs in 1 Kings 22. The prophet Micaiah shares a vision of God to King Ahab that describes an angel being sent to deceive, to satan, the prophet of Ahab:

> 19 Micaiah continued, "Therefore hear the word of the LORD: I saw the LORD sitting on his throne with all the multitudes of heaven standing around him on his right and on his left. 20 And the LORD said, 'Who will entice Ahab into attacking Ramoth Gilead and going to his death there?'
>
> "One suggested this, and another that. 21 Finally, a spirit came forward, stood before the LORD and said, 'I will entice him.'
>
> 22 "'By what means?' the LORD asked.
>
> "'I will go out and be a deceiving spirit (which means to satan) in the mouths of all his prophets,' he said."'You will succeed in enticing him,' said the LORD. 'Go and do it.'

Still another appearance of *the satan* occurs in the book of Job. In ancient Hebrew, *the satan* signifies not the personal name of an angel, but instead a description of its task: in this case to act as the adversary of Job at God's request. In modern biblical translations, however, *the satan* is presented as a personal name by capitalizing the first letter to make "Satan."

Job 1:6–8 describes the "sons of God" presenting themselves before the Almighty. The sons of God are considered angelic manifestations of God of which *the satan* is included. You could look at this as a form of henotheism, with the angels, whose names end with "el" being aspects of or manifestations of ELOHIM as discussed in Chapter 5.

> 6 One day the angels came to present themselves before the Lord, and Satan also came with them. 7 The Lord said to Satan, "Where have you come from?" Satan answered the Lord, "From roaming throughout the earth, going back and forth on it." 8 Then the Lord said to Satan, "Have you considered my servant Job? There is no one on earth like him; he is blameless and upright, a man who fears God and shuns evil."

The satan suggests that Job's faith is not so strong and that he will curse God as soon as things start going bad. God then sends *the satan* out to test Job, saying, "Very well, then, everything he has is in your power, but on the man himself do not lay a finger."

From the Book of Job not only do we receive the notion that *the satan* is an angel, but also that *the satan* is a tempter and adversary of humanity. What we seem to miss is that *the satan* is a "son of God," a manifestation that performs according to the nature of God. *The satan*, according to the Hebrew Bible, does not actually work against God, even if that seems, on the surface, to be the case. This would be the case even if *the satan* believed he opposed God. Nothing is outside of or in true opposition to the Infinite, for there is no other to actually oppose the Infinite.

So how does the idea that *the satan* works for the Infinite fit into the coded *principle* of Genesis? Genesis 3 in its entirety is about self-consciousness, self-absorption, and the consequences thereof, namely: arrogance, shame, blame, guilt, and deceit. Genesis 3 can be understood as entirely the perspective of the deceiver, *the satan*, who has lost its awareness of unity with the Infinite through the dream of self-absorption. *The satan* in Genesis 3 is metaphorically described as the serpent. Let's take a look at Genesis 3 and note the underlined text, which represents the code that is relevant to this chapter.

> Chapter **3:1** And the Nachash[55] was shrewd[56]—from every living thing of the field that YHVH ELOHIM made. And he said toward the woman, "Did ELOHIM indeed say, 'You^P may not eat from any tree of the garden'?" **2** And the woman said toward the Nachash, "From the fruit of the trees of the garden we may eat; **3** and from the fruit of the tree that is in the middle of the garden, ELOHIM said, 'You^P will not eat from it, and you will not touch it, lest you die.'" **4** And the Nachash said toward the woman, "Dying—you^P will not *surely* die![59] **5** For ELOHIM knows that in *the* day you^P eat from it that your eyes will be

---

[55] Heb *nachash*, usually a snake, but it can also refer to a sea creature (Amos 9:3; Isa 27:1), the root meaning "shine" (like brass) or "hiss" as in enchantment.

[56] Heb *'arum*, see previous verse; "nude" comes from the same root, meaning "smooth" or "slick."

[59] Double use of the verb indicates emphasis.

opened and you^P will be as ELOHIM knowing^P good and bad." **6** And the woman saw that the tree *was* good for an eatable *thing*, and that it *was* a longing to the eyes, and the tree *was* desirable for causing insight^c, and she took from its fruit and she ate; and she gave also to her man with her, and he ate. **7** And the eyes of the two of them were opened, and they knew that they *were* nude; and they sewed leaves^s of a fig tree and they made for themselves loin-cloths. **8** And they heard the voice[62] of YHVH ELOHIM walking about in the garden in the wind of the day, and the soil-creature made himself hidden^c—and his woman—from the face^P of YHVH ELOHIM in the middle of the trees^s of the garden. **9** And YHVH ELOHIM called toward the *soil-creature*, and he said to him, "Where *are* you?" **10** And he said, "Your voice I heard in the garden, and I feared, for I *was* nude; and I was hidden." **11** And he said, "Who told to you that you *were* nude? From the tree that I charged you 'so as not to eat from it,' have you eaten?" **12** And the soil-creature said, "The woman, that—you gave her *to be* with me—*she* gave to me from the tree, and I ate." **13** And YHVH ELOHIM said to the woman, "What *is* this you have done?" And the woman said, "The Nachash, he deceived me, and I ate." **14** And YHVH ELOHIM said toward the Nachash, "Because you have done this, cursed *are* you above every animal, and above every living thing of the field; upon your belly you will walk, and dust you will eat, all the days of your life^P. **15** And hostility I will set between you and between the woman, and between your seed and

---

[62] I.e., sound; in Hebrew "voice" is used as a metaphor for all kinds of sounds.

between her seed;[66] *he* will strike you—*on the* head, and *you* will strike him—*on the* heel." **16** Toward the woman he said, "Making abundant[c]—I will *surely* make abundant[c][68]—your distress[69] and your pregnancy; in distress you will bring forth sons, and toward your man[70] *will be* your craving, and *he* will rule in you."[71] **17** And to *Soil-creature*[72] he said, "Because you hearkened to[73] the voice of your woman, and you ate from the tree that I charged you saying, 'You will not eat from it,' cursed *is* the soil on account of you. In distress[74] you will eat it all the days of your life[P]; **18** and thorn and thistle it will sprout for you, and you will eat the plant of the field. **19** In the sweat of your two nostrils you will eat bread, until you return toward the soil, for from it you were taken; for dust you *are,* and toward dust you will return." **20** And the soil-creature called the name of his woman Eve, for *she* was mother of all living. **21** And <u>YHVH ELOHIM</u> made for *Soil-creature* and his woman, robes of skin, and he dressed them. **22** And YHVH ELOHIM said, "Look!—the soil-creature has become like one from us, to know good and bad; and now, lest he send forth his hand and take also from the tree of life[P], and eat, and live for an age . . . !"—**23** And <u>YHVH</u>

---

[66] Or "offspring," Heb *zera'* normally refers to male "seed," but can refer to female reproduction as well (Gen 16:10; Lev 12:2).

[68] Double use of the verb indicates emphasis.

[69] Or "sorrow," same word as v. 17b.

[70] Heb *'ish.*

[71] I.e., with regard to; cf. Gen 4:7, same expression used.

[72] Heb *'adam,* "*soil-creature,*" without the article, probably the proper name, "Adam."

[73] Lit "heard to."

[74] Or "sorrow," "hardship," same word as v. 16.

ELOHIM sent him from the garden of Eden, to service the
soil from which he was taken. **24** And he drove out the soil-
creature, and he made dwell[c] at the east of the garden of
Eden, the cherubim, and the flame of the sword that was
revolving, to guard the way of the tree of life[p].

As you can see, there is a lot to digest in Genesis 3, but don't worry.
It's really not that complicated. Let's look at the first underlined
sentence shown below to begin digesting the coded meaning:

And the Nachash[55] was shrewd[56]—from[57] every living
thing of the field that YHVH ELOHIM made.

This single sentence tells us a lot about the serpent. First, we have
the word Nachash, which on the surface means snake, but has root
meanings of "shine" like brass and "hiss" like an enchantment. The
serpent in the garden is commonly thought of as a physical snake,
but that literal view will not reveal the code. Look at the root
meanings to get a better sense of what is going on here—a shining
enchantment.

The serpent is a metaphor for a compelling feeling or thought
that you can't ignore. In Genesis 3, we can see an enchanting
feeling or thought has taken hold of Eve's mind, not unlike the
thought of a certain comfort food might stick in our minds and
compel us to eat when it's not healthy or necessary to do so. The
same compelling feeling or thought pattern arises in arguments

---

[55] Heb *nachash*, usually a snake, but it can also refer to a sea creature (Amos 9:3;
Isa 27:1), the root meaning "shine" (like brass) or "hiss" as in enchantment.

[56] Heb *'arum*, see previous verse; "nude" comes from the same root, meaning
"smooth" or "slick."

[57] I.e., more shrewd in contrast with ("away from") any other.

when we know we had best not say that certain thing but say it anyway, only to create greater disharmony.

Usually, when we behave in such disharmonious ways, we feel compelled to justify ourselves. If you have experienced that phenomenon, then you have some sense of what Eve is experiencing in Genesis 3.

Prior to eating that comfort food or saying that thing we should not have said, we experienced some inner disharmony potentiating the behavior. The question is, what disharmony set the scene for Eve's behavior? What disharmony within Eve sought comfort?

Notice that the serpent compared Eve to the Infinite, suggesting that she was lacking. The disharmony was a thought in Eve's mind suggesting that she was separate from and less than the Infinite and therefore undeserving of the Infinite's love. Eve judged herself as being bad. Even before the story tells us so, she has already eaten of the tree of the knowledge of good and bad and is suffering the consequence of self-doubt and deceit.

Doubt about self-worth is the first departure from harmony, which a religiously-minded person might call the first sin. The judgment in the case of Eve was "I am not good enough," "I don't measure up," "I don't deserve to be loved." So many of us have felt exactly the same way. These deceptive thoughts and feelings stimulate the search for identity that traps humanity in self-absorption.

For thousands of years, we have been told the original sin, a sin for which humanity as a whole must pay the price, had to do with a young couple eating an apple or a quince against the command of God. We have been told that this sin of disobedience can't be forgiven.

The story is symbolic, much like our dreams. What was consumed was not an actual fruit, but instead, self-judgment and the deceit that one could have the ability to actually measure their essential value. Eve judged herself as being unworthy, which runs against her nature as the embodiment of the Infinite. Nearly all of us consume moral judgment on a daily basis, do we not? It might be self-judgment or judgment of others. In either case, we lose our sense of innocence and the magic of life, and this is what the warning "And from the tree of the knowledge of good and bad, you will not eat from it; for on *the* day you eat from it, <u>dying—you will surely die!</u>" means. Although some would argue that the warning is about physical death, as the story is an allegory, I believe we are wise to look to its deeper spiritual meaning, the death of innocence. The loss of innocence is a form of spiritual death.

Now let's look at the way the serpent tempted Eve, which mirrors the many temptations in our lives. "Dying—youP will not *surely* die!" he said. Do we not sometimes try to convince ourselves that we can get away with deceitful thoughts and behavior? Do we not minimize our misbehavior as just a small, harmless thing that can be hidden or that nobody will notice—that it's no big deal? That is exactly what "Dying—youP will not *surely* die!" means here.

There is always a price to be paid, and there is no getting around it. The price is not always obvious, but it is paid in full through the loss of innocence, life's magic. The serpent represents the devil to whom you have sold your soul.

The first word, "Dying" is the immediate disconnect from reality that is deceit. You might have to go back to the memory of your first big deceit to recall the feeling of tremendous self-absorption at that time. The "not *surely* die" is where the clever mind plays its loose game with reality. The stress on *"surely"* as shown in italics gives us the idea that somehow, we can skirt the law of the Universe, if we are clever enough.

At the level of soul, we get away with absolutely nothing. We pay with the loss of innocence. And when innocence has been crushed out to the degree that our conscience has turned off, then we may no longer even care to justify ourselves. We just do whatever our compulsions tell us to do without a thought of the consequences—a spiritually dark place, indeed.

But let's not repeat the error by blaming Eve, as people have been doing for thousands of years. For the first time in her life, Eve was suffering from self-consciousness. It's like hitting puberty and suddenly being overwhelmed by feelings and urges that you don't understand and can't readily control. The moral judgment wasn't exactly her fault; rather, it was the result of natural evolution and bodily maturation, and the unfounded belief that she could get away with her deceit, that it would go unnoticed, debt unpaid.

Eve then conveyed the feeling of insecurity to Adam and opened his eyes to self-consciousness and moral judgment against himself. In general, girls hit puberty before boys, which is to say they mature more quickly. That's all that is happening here. Eve matured before Adam, which means there is no original sin. Think about how confusing and self-absorbing teen years can be and how all-consuming image-consciousness can be.

Once self-absorption took over, Adam and Eve felt shame at their nakedness and covered their private parts with loincloths made of fig leaves. Now, consider small children, how they can walk around in public naked and feel no shame. So long as children lack self-consciousness, they do not feel shame.

Innocence should not be conflated with certain renunciation practices such as that of Jain monks, who make a statement against comfort and clothing by going nude in public. Renunciation is not innocence. Renunciation, generally speaking, is the abandonment of the pursuit of material comforts with the aim of achieving spiritual enlightenment. Humans do not renounce things until they lose their innocence. I'm not saying that renunciation is wrong. It's just not quite the same thing as innocence.

Genesis 3 tells us of the moment when Adam and Eve lost their innocence through natural maturation and the subsequent development of self-consciousness. What they experienced differs in no essential way from the moment when we became self-conscious and lost our innocence as young children.

For my part, the world felt magical to me until kindergarten, when I took a test for color-blindness. We were not told what the test was for, just that we should look at some colored slides through a lens and call out any numbers we saw within the colored slides. Other children were calling out all the numbers excitedly. I couldn't see a single number, and I began crying, thinking I was stupid. The teacher looked at me at the end of the test and said, "Don't worry about it. There's nothing wrong with you." Her response exacerbated my concern. Obviously, something was wrong with me. I assumed I was lacking in intelligence. Her attempt to downplay my difference only served to confirm my suspicions. We all have had such moments. Maybe it is unavoidable.

Consider how self-consciousness first manifests in our experience. During childhood, we witness people judging themselves or others. And so, we begin to anticipate how we may be judged. We might have been judged for some time before we become conscious enough to anticipate judgment. When we, as young children, have recognized that we can be judged, self-judgment becomes the foundation of our personal identity.

Self-judgment seems to be a natural phase in the socialization process for human beings, which is the spiritual death we discussed earlier with regard to God's warning "dying, you will surely die." When we are just babies, we are simply unable to recognize how others might feel about us or our actions. Without proper socialization, we would be unable to play and cooperate with others, which would be a horrible outcome.

Because humans lack fang, fur, and claw, we require a much greater degree of socialization than do most other animals. Self-consciousness is necessary for the degree of socialization that we require to survive. Self-consciousness may be needed to socialize children so that they will be accepted in the group, but it comes at a price.

Self-judgment hurts deeply, and once it starts, it saps the magic from life. We all fall from innocence when the metaphorical serpent whispers in our ear, "You aren't good enough," "You don't measure up," "You don't deserve love," and we believe it. When that initial deception happens, a disharmony begins to grow within like a malignant cancer, stimulating a search for an identity that makes us feel safe or powerful.

Maybe you can't relate to negative self-judgment, because maybe you feel you are great compared to others. The temptation might be to assume *the principle* does not apply to you in this case. That would be a mistake, for *the principle* covers all forms of self-worth judgments, including those that are comparatively positive. We will get into that aspect of *the principle* more in Part 4.

Here's where the Genesis story becomes a bit counterintuitive. From the myopic perspective of self-absorbed humanity, the serpent seems bad, just as our negative thoughts and judgments seem bad. It helps to remember that nothing is outside of the Infinite, and the Infinite sees everything as good. We just need to open our eyes to see the big picture.

With the idea of an Infinite good in mind, consider the possibility that the serpent in this allegory serves a function of the Infinite. Let us assume that self-judgment is a necessary step in our development. Judgment is the nature of *the satan*; which is to say, judgment is synonymous with *the satan*. You can see from the text above that *the satan* is described as the deceiver and the opposition. The book of Zechariah is where that association begins.

In the book of Zechariah, Joshua, a high priest, is representing the nation of Judah in a trial for its sins. During the trial, God is the judge, while *the satan* is the prosecutor. Below is the relevant passage from Zechariah 3:1:

> 3 "Then he showed me Joshua the high priest standing before the angel of the LORD, and Satan standing at his right side to accuse him."

From the many passages presented thus far in this chapter, we can see *the satan* is described as the adversary, the accuser, a deceiver, a tempter, a prosecutor, and an angel. The association between the qualities of the serpent as *the satan* is obvious. Let's see what happens next in Genesis 3.

> 8 And they heard the voice of YHVH ELOHIM walking about in the garden in the wind of the day, and the soil-creature made himself hidden^c—and his woman—from the face^p of YHVH ELOHIM in the middle of the trees^s of the garden. 9 And YHVH ELOHIM called toward the *soil-creature*, and he said to him, "Where *are* you?" 10 And he said, "Your voice I heard in the garden, and I feared, for I *was* nude; and I was hidden." 11 And he said, "Who told to you that you *were* nude? From the tree that I charged you 'so as not to eat from it,' have you eaten?" 12 And the soil-creature said, "The woman, that—you gave her *to be* with me—*she* gave to me from the tree, and I ate."

In their shame and guilt, Adam and Eve attempt to hide. When God lets on that he knows they have eaten of the tree of the knowledge of good and bad, Adam turns and blames Eve and God simultaneously, for God created Eve and would have known she was going to eat of the tree. Then Eve, wanting to deflect the blame, points to the serpent as the source of the disobedience. Of course, the serpent, like Eve, is also a creation of God, so her blame also reflects back on God.

As a result of self-consciousness, the children now suffer from a trifecta of disharmony—shame, blame, and guilt. God curses all three parties, Eve, Adam, and the serpent:

> **14** And YHVH ELOHIM said toward the Nachash, "Because you have done this, cursed *are* you above every animal, and above every living thing of the field; upon your belly you will walk, and dust you will eat, all the days of your life[p]. **15** And hostility I will set between you and between the woman, and between your seed and between her seed;[66] *he* will strike you—*on the* head, and *you* will strike him—*on the* heel." **16** Toward the woman he said, "Making abundant[c]—I will *surely* make abundant[c]!—your distress and your pregnancy; in distress you will bring forth sons, and toward your man *will be* your craving, and *he* will rule in you."[71] **17** And to *Soil-creature* he said, "Because you hearkened to[73] the voice of your woman, and you ate from the tree that I charged you saying, 'You will not eat from it,' cursed *is* the soil on account of you. In distress[74] you will eat it all the days of your life[p]; **18** and

---

[66] Or "offspring," Heb *zera'* normally refers to male "seed," but can refer to female reproduction as well (Gen 16:10; Lev 12:2).

[71] I.e., with regard to; cf. Gen 4:7, same expression used.

[73] Lit "heard to."

[74] Or "sorrow," "hardship," same word as v. 16.

thorn and thistle it will sprout for you, and you will eat the plant of the field. **19** In the sweat of your two nostrils you will eat bread, until you return toward the soil, for from it you were taken; for dust you *are*, and toward dust you will return."

The response seems like a lot of judgment and cursing from an all-present, all-loving, all-knowing, all-powerful god, one who must have known Adam and Eve would eat of the tree of knowledge of good and bad when "he" created them and placed them in the garden with that seductive tree. The judgment and curses of God seem out of synch with the God represented in Genesis 1. There ELOHIM only saw good.

The key to understanding Genesis 3, to resolving this apparent contradiction, is realizing that every single word therein is a projection of self-absorbed minds. The entire story unfolds from the perspective of the "serpent," the perspective that has lost the sense of unity with *all-that-is*, due to the natural self-absorption that self-consciousness enables. Essentially, the embodied Infinite has forgotten its Infinite nature, and is caught up in personal identification.

Genesis 3 represents, in large part, the evolution of the embodied Infinite, through the enlargement of the human brain, which results in an enhanced degree of self-consciousness and the subsequent judgment that self-consciousness generates. The metaphorical eating of the tree of good and bad represents an evolution in human beings that allows us to realize the specific types of intelligence that differentiate human mental abilities from other animals. We can see the evidence in the following statement from Genesis 3:

"Making abundant[c]—I will *surely* make abundant[d]—your distress and your pregnancy; in distress you will bring forth sons, and toward your man *will be* your craving, and *he* will rule in you."

Many of the reasons that women prior to modernity depended so upon men for survival were biological. First and foremost, until the mid-twentieth century no reliable means of birth control was available, the result of which was that most mature women were nearly constantly pregnant, especially in more primitive circumstances.

The long nine-month gestation period required to prepare a human baby for birth, is far longer than most other animals, with the main exceptions being gorillas (8.5 months), whales (10-14 months), and elephants (about 20 months), all highly intelligent animals that scientists suspect are also self-conscious. During human pregnancy, expectant mothers are highly vulnerable and need protecting and support.

As to the pain of childbirth mentioned in God's curse against women in Genesis 3, the heads of human babies at birth are so large that the width of female hips has necessarily increased over the eons to allow the baby to pass through the birth canal. Biologists largely suggest that the hips of women are already at their maximal evolutionary width. Were the hips to grow much wider, women would lose the ability to walk. Because of the large heads, childbirth is an arduous, painful experience for most women. Of course, if anything goes wrong in the process, the chance of death is much higher than with other animals.

Long gestation periods, the pain and danger of childbirth, the long development cycle of children after birth, with near constant care and mentoring required to raise a healthy functioning human being, combined with the fact that human beings did not have reliable birth control until the 1960s: all of these factors rendered women highly dependent upon their men and the other people in their clans.

Genesis 3 is a description of the natural effects of the evolution of human brains toward enhanced self-consciousness and related mental capacities. With the enhanced self-consciousness that our larger brains provide, coupled with ignorance of our true natures, we condemn ourselves, others, the Universe, and, by proxy, the Infinite almost constantly. Genesis 1-3 warns us that self-absorption is the cause of our suffering.

We have relied almost entirely on our specific flavor of intelligence to survive, specifically by insulating ourselves from nature in ways that other creatures cannot. In the process of protecting ourselves, a psychological separation from our deepest nature, our own bodies, and our felt connection with the Infinite has occurred. In short, we feel deeply alone as a result of the death of innocence.

The fall is not something of the past, but is happening in this very moment, as is the possibility of the return to Eden. To understand this idea, first observe closely the translation below taken from scripture4all.org. It shows the Hebrew (which runs from right to left) and the literal English translation below it that runs from left to right.

3:24 וַיְגָרֶשׁ		אֶת ־ הָאָדָם	וַיַּשְׁכֵּן		מִקֶּדֶם
u·igrsh		ath – e·adm	u·ishkn		m·qdm
and·he-is-driving-out		» the·human	and·he-is-causing-to-tabernacle		from·east

לְגַן	־ עֵדֶן ־ אֶת	הַכְּרֻבִים	וְאֵת	לַהַט	הַחֶרֶב	הַמִּתְהַפֶּכֶת
l·gn	– odn ath – e·krbim		u·ath	let	e·chrb	e·mthephkth
to·garden-of	Eden » the·cherubim		and·»	flame-of	the·sword	the·one-turning-herself

לִשְׁמֹר	אֶת ־ דֶּרֶךְ	עֵץ	הַחַיִּים	: ס
l·shmr	ath – drk	otz	e·chiim	: s
to·to-guard-of	» way-of	tree-of	the·lives	

https://www.scripture4all.org/OnlineInterlinear/OTpdf/gen3.pdf

"and·he-is-driving-out » the·human and·he-is-causing-to-tabernacle from·east to·garden-of Eden » the·cherubim and·» flame-of the·sword the·one-turning-herself to·to-guard-of » way-of tree-of the·lives"

Please note that the Hebrew and the literal translation are in present continuous tense, as can be seen in "He is <u>driving out</u> the human," and "the one-<u>turning</u>-herself." Now read with care to the final English translation:

> 24 So he <u>drove out</u> the man; and he <u>placed</u> at the east of the garden of Eden Cherubims, and a flaming sword which <u>turned</u> every way, to keep the way of the tree of life.

Note that it is entirely portrayed in the past tense with the verbs "drove out," "placed," and "turned." Past tense is an assumed meaning inserted by the translators that results in a very different meaning from the original Hebrew text. If you closely examine the literal translation, in green, directly below the Hebrew text and compare it to the final translation, you will notice that there are a great many assumptions in the translation that can mislead. For our purposes in this chapter, it's enough to notice the change from the correct present continuous tense to the incorrect past tense.

With that simple tense correction in mind, we can see that humanity did not fall irreparably from grace at some distant time in the ancient past. No, it's happening right now, due to the self-absorption we experience in our daily lives. And that message gives us hope, because if self-absorption is causing a sense of separation right now, it means we can do something about it right now, by aiming to be a little less self-absorbed right now and being a little less self-absorbed each day. We now know the path to the tree of life or the "tree of the lives," as it is described above!

To help move us in a healthy direction, spend some time each day taking an account of the moments during the day when you measured or judged your fundamental value or that of another person. Notice when you felt shame, blame, guilt, or arrogance. Let go those feelings, for they are not helpful.

Instead of self-flagellating with ineffectual energies like moral judgment and perpetuating the suffering of Adam and Eve, simply consider what you would prefer in your life if you truly loved yourself and wanted to be the fullest you possible. Do you prefer to continue the behavior that you are judging yourself and others for? If not, do less of it and do a bit more of what takes you in a healthy direction.

By reducing moral judgment, doing less of what is unhealthy for your long-term good, and doing more of what is healthy, your example supports others to make healthy changes as well as to be free of moral judgment. With daily persistence, this practice can bring about tremendous inner clarity and liberation. And remember, there is not, nor was there ever, an original sin.

Chapter 12

The Maps of Life

As we saw in Chapter 9, Genesis 1 maps the perspective of the disembodied Infinite, how it sees the cosmos, the sky, the waters, the earth, the flora, fauna, and humanity as a perfect reflection of itself. Chapter 10 discusses Genesis 2 and how it traces the Infinite's experience of itself through the life of early humans. Genesis 2 tells of an innocent harmonious relationship between humanity and the environment. Chapter 11 reflects on Genesis 3, which underscores the process by which the Infinite experiences individual self-consciousness and self-absorption. As Genesis 3 reflects the current state of humanity, let's take a deeper look at that text's implications.

Genesis 3 functions as a schematic of human consciousness that we can map onto three different processes of human experience. As I suggested, Genesis 2-3 encapsulates the evolutionary process of human beings, going from a more primitive hominid species to homo sapiens, as well as the natural maturation process of childhood development. It also reads as a guide to the meditative or prayer experience. I believe we've spoken enough about the evolutionary map, so, in this chapter let's talk more about the other two maps, the process of childhood development and the process of prayer and meditation. Let's discuss the meditation process first.

As we meditate or pray to sufficient depth, as many people have attested, we are able to encounter the Infinite much as I did when I broke my ankle as a young man. The experience may last minutes, hours, or days before the sense of an isolated self gradually returns. As the pure Infinite experience slips away from us, the feeling of connectedness and communion with our environment remains for a time. It can feel as if everything were alive and conscious at some deeper level, much as Adam and Eve experienced a sense of harmony with themselves, their environment, and the Infinite. At some point, the sense of self returns to some degree and we find ourselves more or less back in our self-absorbed minds, but with a memory of that Infinite experience which serves as a guiding light, helping us open up to the Infinite a bit more in our daily lives.

Readers who have had a direct experience of the Infinite through meditation, prayer, or mystical experience will likely relate to the phases of the process I described above. If you've not had such experiences, you may be able to relate to this part of the Genesis story in another way—through the prenatal and postnatal child development process.

Based on the idea that consciousness, the witnessing capacity, is fundamental, we assume that with a human fetus, the first sense is simply an awareness of being, absent any other sense. At this basic level of development, the person likely has no mental narrative, no inner voice, no sense of a specific self. The feeling of being is boundless because proprioception, a sense that indicates where the borders of the body are relative to the space around it, has yet to develop. Without a sense of borders, you feel indefinite.

As the nervous system further develops, feelings of discomfort stimulate instinctive movement to avoid pain. This instinctive movement refines the brain's awareness of movement. As a result, the fetus might feel all movement—their mother's movement and their own, but remain unable to differentiate the source of the movement. To the fetus, there is probably merely awareness of being, awareness of comfort versus discomfort, and awareness of movement as opposed to stillness. There is no sense of other yet, although awareness of discomfort and movement will eventually lead to that awareness through further development of the central nervous system and brain.

The basic senses of sight, olfaction, taste, and hearing then become a part of the fetus's experience, vague at first, but increasingly stimulating. As these senses develop further, so too does the feeling that some tastes and scents are pleasant while others are unpleasant. Light can be vaguely detected, similar to the way adults can detect light and darkness through closed eyelids. Some sounds feel pleasant, like the voices of parents talking, and others unpleasant, like the sound of an argument. These senses function as if in the background of one's sense of being.

As the nervous system and senses continue developing, the brain, which facilitates increased function, develops a filtering mechanism to limit stimuli so that the fetus is not overwhelmed by the abundance of new sensory information. As the filtering refines, the sense of being dims to make room for the other developing senses, which move to the foreground of attention. The fetus begins to experience a vague sense of self and other.

The brain begins to differentiate the developing body from the mother's body, first through instinctive movement and kinesthetic touch. For example, inside the womb, the fetus might have the feeling of the pressure of their body against the surface of the womb. That sense helps the brain to map out the territory of one's own body as opposed to what is not one's body.

Eventually birth occurs. Now an infant, the brain slowly realizes that what it does not feel inside of itself is not self, but other. An example of this experience might occur if you wake up with what seems to be a stranger's arm on your chest, only to realize after a brief scare that it is actually your own numb limb. Your brain initially assumes that whatever it cannot feel inside is not you. Only when circulation restores feeling to the limb, or if you can calm yourself long enough to think about it for a moment, do you realize that it's your own arm and not actually someone attacking you in your sleep.

The vast array of stimuli found outside the womb enable the senses and the informational filters of the brain to develop still further. Outside the womb, the growing infant generally relies on their eyes to further dial in a physical sense of self. For example, when infant hands first move instinctively in front of their eyes, they must seem like unrecognizable blurs, but as the nervous system feels the movement, which coincides with the blurred objects moving in front of the eyes, the youngster learns how to see and recognize the hands as part of themselves that they can control. This is a well-known phase of developmental anatomy.

Other things begin to attract the eye and inform the person of self and other. Above the crib other blurry objects might hang from the ceiling to entertain. The brain, wanting to experience them, tries to command them to come near as it does with the arms and legs. But unlike the arms and legs, the objects hanging from the ceiling do not obey. The brain might attempt to feel inside of them as it does the body but finds with frustration that it is unable to do so.

Through repeated attempts and failures, reminiscent of a Jedi-reject attempting to telekinetically retrieve a light saber, the brain unconsciously maps out the territory of self and other. This associative process becomes increasingly complex as the nervous system develops through interactions with the body and the environment.

Through the differentiation of self and other, the body learns instinctively to navigate other, which engenders a feeling of control as "your" desire guides the movement more and more, creating a sense of choice. The unconscious movements of instinct, while still occurring, are no longer the only type of movement.

The sense of self develops still further as the child experiences more control over their body and the environment. For example, the child discovers that they seem to be able to choose some of their experiences, selecting what they like and avoiding dislikes. They also learn to use their voice to call to parents. Eventually the growing self learns to refine those calls, which gives even more control over the environment and experience.

Now a child can say, "I am me."

As children develop, they become familiar with their strengths and weaknesses, proclivities, and place in society. They also develop impressions and opinions about themselves, others, and the world.

Feelings, thoughts, and words swarm the mind to reinforce the developing sense of self until it appears totally real. Yet, a subtle feeling of undifferentiated being may linger. That feeling is the source of the innocence and awe young children feel—a sense that almost everyone loses by the time they enter puberty.

The first hints of the serpent's seductive voice usually show up somewhere around age three or four, as we learn to distort people's sense of reality by telling stories or by lying to gain advantage or to escape consequences such as punishment. The storytelling ability is a requirement for self-absorption, and human beings are instinctive story tellers, which is to say, we are captivated by stories. By the time puberty hits, the judging serpent voice is speaking to us regularly, judging ourselves, others, and the moment as good or bad.

As the sense of self develops further, it is modified by socialization and experiences with parents, neighbors, friends, school, ethnicity, culture, talents, higher education, knowledge, career, and the greater society. Knowledge of personal strengths and weaknesses develops through interactions with our environment and the many accumulated judgments about ourselves, others, and the world around us. Judgment begins to define our story of self.

At this stage of life, the person feels quite capable as a human being, at least compared to infancy. But through the developmental process, they might recognize something important was lost—the simple sense of being. That sense is the magic of life.

So, as you can see through the processes of pre- and post-natal development: your life begins with undifferentiated awareness, then transforms into childlike innocence through the development of the senses and basic human capacities. That state then personalizes more via the development of self-consciousness and socialization, until one is completely absorbed in the story of their own life.

Through this process, the person develops greater functionality and capacity to navigate the world, but loses touch with the innate sense of connection with life. The development of self-consciousness is not a mistake, nor is it a sin. Self-consciousness and the disharmony that comes with it are necessary parts of the maturation of the embodied Infinite as it moves toward the next phase of evolution, the awakening.

Intermission

We have reached a pivotal point of the book. Before we move on, I want to share the teaching philosophy of my martial arts instructor, Osaki Shizen, as I believe it may be helpful to readers now.

When I trained in the Samurai arts with my teacher, he explained very little about technical aspects. He would demonstrate and talk about the form of the techniques, but he never explained the underlying principles. If asked, he simply repeated what he had already told me.

With regard to his teaching method, he explained that he wanted his students to develop high levels of awareness, and that if he explained how to do everything it would result in dull minds, lacking the necessary awareness to take the arts to the next level.

For years, I trained in this way, not really knowing what I was doing. Eventually, I became a bit sharper and more capable, so he gave me instructor's licenses in the four arts that he had taught me. At that time, he explained his teaching philosophy in more depth.

His aim was for students to develop such heightened awareness during their exploration of the arts that they would eventually surpass his abilities. Training in this way would allow the arts to grow deeper with each generation. He said:

> *If I explain my theories to you, you would likely follow exactly the approach that I use and therefore not discover anything new. I believe in you and think you can take it to the next level. When you train your students, please have faith in their abilities to surpass you. In this way, the arts will continue to prosper.*

I rather liked this idea because I understood that it was the approach that Einstein used to learn physics. Instead of following his professors' methods, as students of his time were encouraged to do, Einstein challenged himself to prove difficult theorems in his own way. Surely, his dedication to self-discovery helped prepare him to formulate his revolutionary theory of relativity.

With the mindset of self-discovery, I would like to draw your attention back to the code. After reading the first three parts, do you believe you can see it? Can you articulate it concisely, so that someone else could understand it? Are you able to identify *the principle* that the code reveals and explain it in a functional way? If you've truly seen the code, you should be able to predict with a high degree of accuracy how to unlock the metaphorical gates of Eden. You might take a few minutes to try to explain it in writing or aloud to yourself.

If you are having difficulties articulating the code or *the principle*, or you feel gaps remain in your understanding, please consider giving yourself some time to feel your way through the material with the aim of articulating both the code and *the principle*. In doing so, maybe you will see beyond what I have written so far.

Wouldn't that be wonderful? Of course, if you would prefer to read on without reflecting in this way, you are welcome to do so.

To help clarify the content of Part 3, on the next page, I have also included an insightful song that I hope you will enjoy. To get the greatest benefit, I recommend listening to the song as you read the lyrics. You can listen for free by searching YouTube for "The Brothers Reed Irish Hymn."

Irish Hymn

The Brothers Reed

You asked me to be and here I am...
An indistinct whisper without even a chance...
An instinct desire to be remembered but can't....
Despite all frustrations I've made peace with that.

The devil said "hey boy, well what have you got?"
"I ain't got no pockets, just holes in my socks."
He said "let me tell you the secret to life....
One bite from my apple and I'll help you survive."

Oh Lord please, I'm down on my knees
In a world of confusion with answers to seek.
Hungry and weak with nothing to lose,
I'd like to see you spend a day in my shoes.

Go on and take me, I'm ready I am.
Or are you just a child playing in the sand?
I'll welcome the waves to bring me back in...
and I'll rest on the bottom in silence content.

Oh Lord please, I'm down on my knees
In a world of confusion with answers to seek.
Hungry and weak with nothing to lose,
I'd like to see you spend a day in my shoes.

Part 4

The Book of God

One of the central tenets of Judaism and Christianity is the understanding that God is completely whole. Being completely whole, God neither comes from, nor depends upon anything else. Because of perfect wholeness, God is complete and therefore unchanging.

A common idea among Christians holds that the Infinite changed the rules by making a new promise to humanity with the coming of Jesus. The belief in a new promise is a false belief because the Infinite, being whole and complete, does not change. In fact, we have no promise from the Infinite whatsoever, for the Infinite is not manipulative or coercive. Only the self-absorbed make such conditional deals.

Many believers might wonder what the above paragraph says about the relationship between human beings and the Infinite. A way to understand that relationship is to see human beings as the dream of the Infinite, not something outside of or beneath it. Within the human experience, one generally does not realize the wholeness at the foundation of human existence.

Exceptional individuals have lived among us from time to time who realize their foundational unity. In the past, those exceptional people were considered avatars, masters, prophets, et cetera. Let's set aside those titles, for those labels do not bring clarity. Those people are just like anyone else, except that somehow they maintained a sense of their innate nature. I suspect that sense will soon become much more common among human beings.

As I suggested in Part 1, consciousness is the ground from which the hologram of "reality" emerges. As such, it's important not to get that relationship conceptually turned around: if we think of consciousness as a part of or an aspect of reality, that distorts our perception of consciousness. The error would be to think of consciousness as a thing *within* reality, when it is actually no-thing. To minimize the mind's tendency to view consciousness in that limited way, we will describe consciousness through perceptual possibilities.

Consciousness has two simultaneous primary perceptual possibilities. First, we have the infinite perspective, which, henceforth, I will call "Pure Consciousness" or capital C "Consciousness." Then there is the finite perspective, which I will call "Universal Mind" or capital M "Mind."

Pure Consciousness, the ground of all existence, is totally inclusive of all possibilities. As a result of being totally open in perspective, its awareness does not get caught up in the details of any particular possibility or self.

Universal Mind, on the other hand, experiences selves that seem finite. As a result of the seeming finite experiences, its awareness tends to get caught up in the details. The finite, by definition, is temporary, has an end, does not last. Yet both the infinite and the finite are perspectives of unified being.

Getting a very basic understanding of these two perspectives will help us to better understand our own lives and how we might find balance. In Part 4, we will explore the nature of the Witness through both Consciousness and Mind perspectives and link them back to our reading of YHVH ELOHIM as seen in Genesis.

In Chapter 13, we explore the mysterious infinite perspective of Pure Consciousness and relate it back to the tetragrammaton (YHVH) based on the Hebrew meaning of that word and the relevant mystical experience detailed in Chapter 2.

In Chapter 14, we analyze the enigmatic finite perspective of what I call Universal Mind (ELOHIM) and develop the understanding that what we think of as reality is actually an enjoyable stream of consciousness, a revelation even to the Witness.

In Chapter 15, we explore the mystery of what is variously called the Holy Spirit or the Word of God, and reveal how it relates to Pure Consciousness, Universal Mind, the Universe, and you.

And in Chapter 16, we discuss the perspective and path of the individual who is awakening to their essential nature. We will cover the many challenges along the path and consider the corrective schematic that the code and *principle* of *no other* provides.

Note: in the coming chapters, I describe various aspects of the Witness (God), using new terminology, such as Pure Consciousness and Universal Mind. These new indicators as well as the two prior indicators, Infinite and Witness, all refer to the same Immeasurable Being. I have capitalized each indicator to remind the reader that they indicate different aspects or ways of seeing the same thing.

Chapter 13

Pure Consciousness

As stated in the introduction to Part 4, the Infinite has two primary perspectives: Pure Consciousness and Universal Mind. This chapter examines the perspective of Pure Consciousness, the unchanging ground from which all perceived change stems.

People who have experienced Pure Consciousness tend to describe it as feeling infinitely more meaningful than ordinary reality. The feeling gives a sense of being completely present and ineffable. I believe the ineffability of the experience led to the creation of the tetragrammaton, what you might recognize as יהוה (YHVH) in the Hebrew Bible. In modern Bibles this symbol is typically rendered as "Lord." Modern Jewish teachings state that YHVH is the personal name of ELOHIM (God).

We can look to the tetragrammaton YHVH to get a sense of the characteristics of YHVH, as ancient Jewish naming focused on describing the characteristics of an individual and their reputation.

Although we can get some hints as to the characteristics of the Divine through the naming scheme, we can't get the pronunciation that way.

The issue with determining the proper pronunciation is that ancient Hebrew is thought to be a sacred language that was not spoken in the past. The alternative is that it was once a spoken language, but the people lost the ability to speak it thousands of years ago. Either way, we cannot be sure of pronunciation. This turn of events was due to the Jewish people having no country of their own for centuries. Being spread out among different cultures in the Middle East and Europe, ancient Hebrew, if it ever was a spoken language was lost when Jewish people began speaking Yiddish and Ladino, trade languages which mix Hebrew and the languages of the Northern European and Mediterranean countries in which they lived.

Although the written Hebrew remained intact, we can't be sure of the pronunciation, because the Hebrew language doesn't contain vowels. Without vowels, it's not possible to accurately reconstruct the spoken language from the text alone. To establish a standard for pronunciation, Jewish rabbis and scribes later consulted the Greek records of Hebrew scripture which contain vowels. Of course, there was no way to be sure the Greek pronunciation of Jewish scripture accurately reflected the ancient Jewish pronunciation, but it was the only option. As a result, no one really knows the original Hebrew pronunciation of YHVH.

Although we may never know the original Hebrew pronunciation of YHVH, we can get a sense of the characteristics of the divine through the Hebrew characters that make up the tetragrammaton. This is so because the Jewish naming scheme is meant to reflect characteristics of what is named, and this naming scheme was applied to the tetragrammaton. That said, the characteristics indicated by the tetragrammaton give anyone who understands Hebrew a sense that the tetragrammaton is not actually meant to be understood intellectually.

The letters of the tetragram are associated with the Hebrew root for "existence." Translated into English, we get "to be." These meanings reflect the ever-present nature of the Witness. English speakers might associate it with the statement "I AM that I AM," in the story of Moses and the burning bush.

In Exodus 3:14, Moses asks YHVH how he should reply to the Israelites when they ask which God has sent him to them. YHVH replied that he should tell them "I AM that I AM," and that "I AM has sent me to you." The statement carries a sense of non-comparison, as if there is no other to compare to.

The key point here is that the root words that make up YHVH are hints of its impersonal nature. To think of it as the personal name of God is a profound misunderstanding. YHVH is not a name, but instead a hint of the ineffable. We should also be careful to note that ELOHIM also isn't a name but a generalized term for deities. Similarly, our English "God" is a stand in for ELOHIM. Neither God nor ELOHIM were meant to be names.

To modern religious Jews, the name of God is considered too sacred to utter and pronouncing the tetragrammaton (YHVH) is blasphemous. To avoid blasphemy, they typically substitute the word "Adonai," which means "Lord", to avoid saying "Yahveh" or "Yehovah." But ultra-orthodox Rabbis consider Adonai too holy to say, so the practice in their communities is to say, "Ha-Shem," which means "The Name."

Consider the image that Adonai (Lord) conjures in the mind. It conjures the image of a king, does it not? The image seems tangible and personal. This mental idol bears no resemblance to the actuality of YHVH.

Ha-Shem (The Name) is similarly misleading, for it assumes that God is personal and has a name. Both of these ideas can act as false idols that veil the individual who entertains them from the direct experience of Pure Consciousness.

Substituting Adonai or Ha-Shem for the tetragrammaton is a long tradition in Judaism, but I suspect the original reason for the substitution has been lost. The most commonly stated reason for not pronouncing the name comes from Deuteronomy 5:11, which is the third of the ten commandments: "You shall not misuse the name of the Lord your God, for the Lord will not hold anyone guiltless who misuses his name."

I do not believe the third commandment led to the rule against uttering the tetragrammaton because banning casual use of the name does not mean the same as not using it at all. I suspect the inability to effectively convey the experience of Pure Consciousness has led to the dogmatic use of Adonai or Ha-Shem. To clarify what I suspect is the original reason for not pronouncing the tetragrammaton, let's reflect back on the transcendent experience detailed in Chapter 2.

During that mystical experience of Pure Consciousness, any attempt on my part to define it felt viscerally wrong. And any attempt to speak those formulations felt even more wrong. The very thought of definition resulted in what I can best describe as being shushed by the cosmos and my own body. I was left in crystal clear silence.

Experiences of Pure Consciousness can vary in intensity. The more intense the experience, the less there remains a sense of a personal self to mentally filter and define the experience. If the intensity of the experience is so great that no personal you seems to exist in the experience, there will be unspeakable revelation without thought. At lower intensities, the personal you may still be there, cognizant to a degree that would seem to suggest that you could name or define the Infinite. My reference to Pure Consciousness in this chapter denotes high intensity experiences where the personal self has become thin or non-existent.

During my first experience of Pure Consciousness, my personal self seemed present but rather quiet. The lingering personal perspective explains why I saw myself as separate from Pure Consciousness despite its conveyance that we were one and the same. Let's revisit that experience at the point where I tried to name or define it, as naming is especially relevant to this chapter.

Because of the desire to convey the experience, I felt compelled to come up with some indicator for the Infinite, without using the loaded word "God," which conjures an image of an old, bearded man on a cloud for so many people. The fact that I avoid calling Pure Consciousness "God" sometimes offends people. My avoidance of the term is well-reasoned and is never meant to offend anyone. I simply feel that the term God is too loaded with unhelpful associations to be useful these days. Avoiding the term God does not offend Pure Consciousness, for it is not self-absorbed.

Regarding associated meanings, it seems to me that frequently no two people have identical associations with common words, let alone the most charged word in the human language—God. Even if our mental definitions are the same, our feelings behind those definitions can vary widely.

To ease communication, I tried to come up with a term to accurately portray the wholeness of Pure Consciousness. The best one I could arrive at was the least defined. It simply IS with no qualifiers, and so I began calling it variously Isness or Beingness.

Several decades later, when I researched the meaning of the tetragrammaton (YHVH), I was shocked to find that it intimates "Being," or "Existing." Sadly, for me, those words along with Isness and Beingness fail. Because the Infinite exists and is beyond existence simultaneously, to say that it IS, conveys only a half-truth. Truly, Pure Consciousness transcends measuring and defining. The best strategy, I felt, was to use the least loaded, least misleading words available, even if they were at best half-truths. There doesn't seem to be a perfect solution. With that guideline in place, Isness, Beingness, Being, and Existing will have to do, for they are the closest we can get with language.

I greatly appreciated the tetragrammaton when I first encountered it in my research because of its intimated meaning, "Being," or "Existing." As the mind is incapable of fully understanding those words, I saw clearly that the tetragrammaton was never meant to be fully understood. I felt the tetragrammaton was in perfect alignment with the best words I could choose, "Isness," and "Beingness."

With regard to the tetragrammaton (YHVH), it's best not to think of it as a name, but instead as an indicator of something that defies names or precise descriptions. No word will ever truly describe its nature. We are wise to be honest about the limitations of our measurements, definitions, and comprehension, for even the Witness does not understand. For me, any name applied to Pure Consciousness feels viscerally inaccurate in every cell of my body. That powerful feeling of inaccuracy is likely shared by anyone who has had the full experience. I suspect that feeling of error associated with trying to define Pure Consciousness gave rise to both the formation of the tetragrammaton and the subsequent prohibition against pronouncing it.

Let's imagine that a religious leader directly experiences Pure Consciousness and subsequently tells people that naming this phenomenon is viscerally wrong. Not naming Pure Consciousness then becomes a rule within the religion. If the reason for the rule is not sufficiently explained, however well meaning, the rule will have the opposite effect of what was intended.

The original use of the tetragrammaton indicated that the Infinite can't be intellectually understood or defined. In fact, if while having the experience you attempt to name or define it, the mental activity stimulates disharmony between your mind and body, which may lessen your clarity of the experience or pull you from it entirely. It helps to remember the guideline provided by Psalm 46:10 to "Be still, and know that I am God."

The rule against pronouncing YHVH gives cause for judging the self or others, and that creates unnecessary disharmony. When we judge, our hearts close, and that feeds our sense of separation from the Infinite. The unintended effect of the ban on speaking this word thus seems to produce the exact opposite of the intention behind the original rule, which presumably was to draw people closer to the Infinite.

A related false belief centers on the idea that the Infinite can be offended. This belief makes people feel fearful and nervous, resulting in an even greater sense of division from the Infinite. Pure Consciousness is not a personal perspective, so it does not take offense to anything. When we take into account all the disharmony that the rule causes, it seems preferable to discard the rule and admit that the tetragrammaton is not a name.

No matter which word we use to indicate the Infinite, generally speaking, it's most important to remember that there is no actual other. Pure Consciousness is our nature, whether we consciously perceive it or not. Returning to Psalm 46:10: "Be still, and know that I am God," whenever you see the tetragrammaton or any word indicating the foundation of being, you might pause and become vibrantly silent for a few seconds. Practicing in this way is very helpful.

Taking it further, practicing vibrant silence in your daily life can reveal a sense of the ever-present moment that can be tremendously transformational in your life. The key is pausing to experience the vibrant presence of the moment and noticing what prevents you from fully entering that experience. If you work to correct the blockages while practicing vibrant silence, over time, the experience becomes more accessible. Eventually your life becomes the conscious embodiment of vibrant presence.

A person who experiences the fullness of Pure Consciousness is likely to perceive a pure white or possibly golden light. Because the infinite perspective is all inclusive, our brains will likely perceive it as white. It seems that the brains perception of a gold light during experiences of Pure Consciousness comes from the natural association between gold and absolute purity. I do not believe Pure Consciousness actually has a specific color, but white or gold is how the visual cortex is likely to experience it. On a feeling level, due to its total openness, the experience of Pure Consciousness would be vibrant present clarity, enveloping love, total acceptance, and a sense of perfect wholeness.

Although it is quite rare for a human to experience Pure Consciousness, those who do tend to wish they could live there eternally. When they return to normal awareness, many such individuals dedicate the rest of their lives trying to get back to it, to understanding it, or to sharing paths that assist others to experience it.

The prodigious Russian novelist, Fyodor Dostoevsky, who suffered from seizures, often experienced what sounds like Pure Consciousness just before the onset of an intense seizure. Dostoevsky wrote about his ecstatic seizures through one of his characters, Prince Myshkin, in *The Idiot*: "I feel complete harmony in myself and in the world and this feeling is so strong and sweet that for several seconds of such bliss one would give ten years of one's life, indeed, perhaps one's whole life."

I felt similarly while experiencing Pure Consciousness the first time. If it were possible to bottle Pure Consciousness and give it away, I would have spent my life in a bottling plant. Now I realize that's not the way. Most people, if they knew what they would have to sacrifice through the experience, would not drink it. Still others would label those who drank it drug users, and before long there would be laws against it. People find myriad ways of avoiding Pure Consciousness.

The key point to keep in mind is that we have no way to intellectually understand Pure Consciousness, but we can feel it. It can be experienced. And no matter how often you make mistakes in your life, it helps to know that there is nothing you could ever say or do to offend the Infinite, for it does not see you as separate from itself.

Here is a healthy exercise that I recommend you spend a few minutes per day practicing. Make yourself comfortable and close your eyes. Imagine that beneath or behind your perception of the world a brilliant white light unifies everyone and everything in unconditional love.

Don't overthink this exercise. Make no effort to analyze or turn this practice into a philosophy or ideology. Instead, allow yourself to be innocent like a young child during this exercise. Imagine the entire Universe aglow with a warm, embracing love. Imagine your body also suffused with this light. Release all judgment against yourself, your body, others (including your enemies), and the Universe. Be with love to the extent that you can for just a few minutes each day.

With practice you will be able to do this with your eyes open, but for many people, it's easier to begin with closed eyes. You might try it both ways each day to train the brain to be flexible.

Chapter 14

Universal Mind

In Chapter 13, we discussed Pure Consciousness, or the Witness' infinite perspective. In this chapter, we'll explore the potential for Mind within the Witness. The Mind of the Witness shares many qualities in common with the human mind, which we examine later. Moving forward, to avoid confusion about which mind I am referring to, I will refer to the mind of the Witness as Universal Mind.

Universal Mind is the perspective through which the Witness projects the torus-shaped holograms described in Chapter 3. In this chapter, I will expand upon the mystical experiences in Chapter 2 (The Infinite) and Chapter 3 (The Face of God) to deepen our understanding of the nature of Universal Mind.

You might recall from Chapter 3 (The Face of God) that I felt confused about how the Infinite saw no difference between myself and itself. I, on the other hand, could not see myself as being it. I wondered how I could have a separate identity and not be aware of my true nature, which is Infinite. I received the answer, but I did not understand until several decades later. Here is what I was shown that I did not convey in Chapter 2 or Chapter 3.

Upon asking about the enigma, my attention was directed to a tiny clouded space which appeared much like a nebula, a cluster of interstellar clouds illuminated by starlight. My mind zoomed into that nebula-like formation and saw its workings. While zooming in, I could see that within Pure Consciousness is the possibility of Universal Mind, or that clouded nebula-like space. Universal Mind could be understood as the potential for Pure Consciousness to play a game with itself, by imagining itself through equal and opposite definitions, one positive and one negative as I described in Chapter 3.

Universal Mind exists as a stream of consciousness that spontaneously projects interdependent and opposite ideas about its nature. To give you an idea of what I saw, imagine what we see of our Galaxy through the Hubble Telescope—more stars than there are grains of sand on all the beaches of our planet. And we also know that there are galaxies beyond the Milky Way as plentiful as the stars in our galaxy. I saw universes just as plentiful, birthing and dying, birthing and dying, endlessly. All of that was shown to me in just a few minutes.

The primary difference between Pure Consciousness and Universal Mind, from my point of view, is that Pure Consciousness is totally centered and clear, whereas Universal Mind is, for lack of a better term, excited in its play. Universal Mind spontaneously projects concepts that it explores. Each projection contains the essences of both Universal Mind and Pure Consciousness. The Mind within each projection explores its nature, playfully seeking to understand itself. In this way, each projection creates offspring projections which are extrapolations of its parent projection. With each offspring, Mind begins to lose track of its basis in Pure Consciousness, resulting in a lack of clarity, which causes the nebula-like cloudiness that I was shown.

Pure Consciousness and Universal Mind are both wonderful, awe-inspiring experiences. Both are truly immeasurable, but Universal Mind as it extrapolates with each generation progressively loses awareness of its immeasurable nature and enjoys playing with what seems measurable. With the progressive fading of contextual awareness, the desire to define the undefinable and measure the immeasurable expands.

The two potentials or aspects of the Witness, Pure Consciousness and Universal Mind, map onto the viewing modes of our eyes. Peripheral vision takes in the entire visual field to see the big picture, but it is not good for seeing fine details. Foveal vision is focused and able to see in fine detail, but it lacks contextual awareness. Pure Consciousness is peripherally aware, which means that it sees all potential. Universal Mind, on the other hand, loses that peripheral awareness as it becomes more involved in the play of specific possibilities.

Universal Mind, relative to the brilliant light of Pure Consciousness, is dark. Universal Mind's nature is to project speculations about itself. Self-definition clouds Universal Mind, leading to even more projections of its nature.

Universal Mind is a completely contained, energy efficient, perpetual motion system. Through its many layers of projections, Universal Mind gets lost in self-definition, just as you tend to do in your dreams. The result is a perpetually recurring loop, the torus.

Reading this, you might think the experience of Universal Mind is unpleasant, but the opposite is true. Universal Mind is an orgasmic state of innocent self-exploration. The Witness is having fun! And from its perspective, everything is very, very good.

Universal Mind is memory, and memory is the perception of time. Time is the story of life. Pure Consciousness does not identify with the story of life, which means it is not bound by time. Pure Consciousness is the eternal moment.

To summarize, Universal Mind projects a spontaneous stream of interdependent opposing speculations of its nature. They are always dualistic because the projections cannot be perceived without equal and opposite projections. A torus is generated from the tension between the two opposing forces. A dream of reality is experienced by Universal Mind as it explores the projections of its nature.

All holograms of Universal Mind (what we perceive as reality) contain three common forces. The first is the apparent desire to explore the nature of the self. The second is the instability and excitement that this desire causes. The third is the compulsion to find balance within an ever-changing system. These three forces stimulate a universal game of musical chairs, where projections within Universal Mind keep seeking self-understanding but never finding it because the truth of the ever-present moment can never be fully understood. Universal Mind joyfully continues playing.

Through infinite generations of extrapolation, Universal Mind experiences vivid detail. As detail becomes ever more vivid, expanded, and seemingly personal, Universal Mind tends to get caught up in its dreams, believing it is its projections. The experience of a human being represents the captured state of mind. When absorbed in this way, Universal Mind believes it is a person (small 'm' mind) who is somehow separate from everything else.

The playful projection of opposites fuels the generation of still more generations of exploration within the mind of a human being. Were it not for these projections of your mind, you could not see, could not move, could not function in any way within the hologram we think of as reality. Your thoughts are all interdependent dual projections that paint a more or less functional map of your accessible sensory reality. You are the image and likeness of the Witness. There is no other.

The experience of Universal Mind does not become unpleasant until it explores self-consciousness through life-forms like human beings. As humans are the embodiment of the Witness, we might recall that so long as desire to identify and believe in our definitions of self persists, our mind has no choice: it defines, it contrasts, and it gets lost. Being lost can be great fun, but it can also lead to compulsive suffering that spins itself in circles trying to define and control what is beyond definition and control.

A healthy exercise that you might actively apply throughout your day is to notice whenever you label yourself as being this or that. The most obvious such labels to notice are when you label yourself as being "good" or "bad." But any label that you really identify with, such as your job title, your social or economic position, your worthiness, et cetera, all deserve attention. Just as importantly, you might note resistance to any labels that you strongly identify against, such as "I'm not a liar" or "I'm not stingy." Maintaining such labels can be very limiting and prevent healthy life improvement.

You might also take note of when you lock others into labels. It's so easy to do. When we believe others are the labels that we have psychically attached to them, it becomes very difficult for those people to break free without severing the relationship. Set them free by disbelieving the labels. In your heart, you might discount even the labels that they apply to themselves.

The aim of this exercise is to touch base with your essential, undefined nature little by little throughout your day. When you notice a label arise in your mind, take note of it and remind yourself that in essence you are *no thing* in particular. Allow yourself a moment to feel what it is to be without any thought. Even a few seconds here and there helps.

Of course, if you are still enjoying your game of self-defining, you might continue playing. If you'd prefer another path, you might begin the practice of non-labeling. Whatever you choose, it's all good.

Chapter 15

The Holy Spirit

In Chapters 13 and 14, we decoded the meanings of YHVH and ELOHIM in as much detail as possible. Because of their immeasurable nature, any description can at best be only a half-truth. That said, even a half-truth, so long as we remain aware that it is a half-truth, can be enough to spark a powerful transformation in our lives and open us up to a greater experience of unity. To go further in our understanding, we need to decode another perspective of the Witness, the Holy Spirit.

The Holy Spirit, otherwise known as the "spirit of ELOHIM" first appears in the opening of Genesis 1. To connect with this sense of the Holy Spirit, it helps to view Genesis 1 as an anthropomorphized allegorical explanation of the dreaming process of ELOHIM through the interdependent opposite forces of existence, non-existence, darkness and light, day and night.

(Bere'sheet)

1 At *the* first[2] of ELOHIM[3] creating the skies and the land —
2 and the land was[4] desolation and emptiness; and
darkness *was* over *the* face[p] of *the* deep, and <u>the spirit[5] of
ELOHIM was hovering[6] over the face of the waters</u> — **3** and
ELOHIM said, "Let there be light"; and it was light. **4** And
ELOHIM saw the light, that *it was* good; and ELOHIM
separated between the light and between the darkness.
5 And ELOHIM called to the light "day," and to the
darkness he called "night." And it was evening and it was
morning — day one.

Initially, in "creating" the skies and the land, there is desolation,
emptiness, and darkness in the deep. These descriptions represent
the void space from which the dream of "objective reality" springs
forth. The sky and the land represent the beginning of the
dreaming process, where a mental juxtaposition emerges between
"heaven" and "earth."

This chapter explains the mystery of the Holy Spirit in three
ways: by connecting it to the concept of the Word of God ("Logos")
as it is referenced in John 1:1, as it was shown to me in mystical

---

[2] Lit "At *the* head of," Heb *Bere'sheet* in this grammatical construction is a temporal
phrase meaning, "When at first . . .," see Jer 26:1 where the same form occurs.
It presents the "state of things" when the creative activity begins.

[3] ELOHIM is a plural noun, but often functions as a collective singular, taking a
singular verb. It is related to the Hebrew terms: *'eloah* and *'el*, meaning God,
god, power, or mighty one, and can refer to judges and leaders, heavenly
beings, the gods of the nations, or the one God of Israel.

[4] Or "became."

[5] Heb *ruach*, lit "wind," see Gen 7:1.

[6] I.e., "fluttering," or "shaking," see Deut 32:11; Jer 23:9, the only two other places
this verb is used, always in an intensive form (Piel).

experience, and as it relates to current scientific findings of the Universe. Let's look at John 1:1 first.

> 1 In the beginning was the Word, and the Word was with God, and the Word was God. 2 He was with God in the beginning. 3 Through him all things were made; without him nothing was made that has been made. 4 In him was life, and that life was the light of all mankind. 5 The light shines in the darkness, and the darkness has not overcome it.

When I received the vision that I affectionately call "The Face of God" (Chapter 3), I was stunned at the unimaginably pure positivity that appeared to vibrate from the Witness as it projected the polarities of possibilities which are the tori we perceive as reality. You'll notice in the introduction to Genesis 1, it says "the spirit of ELOHIM was hovering over the face of the waters." If you look at Dr. Tabor's note for "hovering," you will see that the alternate meanings for hovering are fluttering or shaking. This fluttering or shaking is a vibration over the face of the torus.

The best way I can describe that vibration is as a song of eternal loving praise that rippled out from the center like endless back-to-back concentric rings that moved along the surface of the torus like a great wind over a field of tall grass. Witnessing this phenomenon, I understood the essence of the *Holy Spirit* and the *Word of God* to be one and the same. John 1:1 opens with "In the beginning was the Word, and the Word was with God, and the Word was God."

Let's take a deeper look at those words, which begin with reference to *bere'sheet*, which is a Hebrew word typically translated as "In the Beginning." Bere'sheet is the title of the first book of the

Hebrew Bible and is written in the opening of the first sentence of the Hebrew Bible. This repetition alludes to its importance.

Bere'sheet is the Alpha and the Omega, the beginning and the end. As a title, Bere'sheet is translated in English as "Genesis." Clearly, the word bere'sheet is pivotal to gaining a functional understanding not only of this chapter, but Genesis 1-3, reality, and our own natures, at least to the degree that any of these things can be understood.

If you have a sufficiently deep understanding of the timeless meaning of bere'sheet, you will quickly recognize the areas of The Holy Bible that go astray, just as you will quickly see the areas within yourself and your life that are astray.

Bere'sheet is made up of two Hebrew words, *Bet* (ב) and Roshe (ראש). The combination has a number of possible meanings, which potentially allow our minds to select meanings that are not in alignment with the principle. *Bet* is a general good-for-all-purposes preposition that could mean "in," "at," "with," "among," "during," "by," et cetera. The root word Roshe is made up of the Hebrew letters: Resh, Alef, and Shin. Roshe as it is commonly used means *beginning* or *head*. When we look at Strong's Concordance and Lexicon, the go-to source for research on biblical Hebrew, we find the following information:

> rô'sh, roshe; from an unused root apparently meaning to shake; the head (as most easily shaken), whether literal or figurative (in many applications, of place, time, rank, etc.): — band, beginning, captain, chapter, chief(-est place, man, things), company, end, × every (man), excellent, first, forefront, (be-)head, height, (on) high(-est part, (priest)), × lead, × poor, principal, ruler, sum, top.
>
> https://www.blueletterbible.org/lexicon/h7218/kjv/wlc/0-1/

As you can see, Hebrew is a complex language in which one root word could have many possible related meanings. Such complexity renders it easy to misapprehend an intended meaning. To limit misunderstanding as much as possible, I will use three guides to corral it: the actual Hebrew definitions according to Strong's Concordance and Lexicon, mystical experiences of the Infinite, and relevant scientific findings.

Because Genesis, to date, has been interpreted through the lens of time, "In the beginning" is the traditional translation. If we remove time from the equation, we must consider other possible meanings to determine which, if any, fit with the code.

Many readers might think "the highest" would work, but it doesn't because *the highest* is a comparative statement that does not fit with "there is no other." Remember, it takes two to compare. To label the Infinite as the "highest" is to judge everything else as below it, which is the errant perspective of Adam and Eve in Genesis 3.

Our minds tend to think of the Infinite as being above us, precisely because we have judged ourselves as being ungodly, as did Adam and Eve. To keep ourselves from falling into this trap, let's keep the all-is-one, all-is-good, all-is-God perspective of the Witness as our guide.

Now that we've ruled out "the highest," let's look at other possible translations to see what might work. Fortunately, the code gives us clear guidelines for our selection. Because we are referring to the non-dual Pure Consciousness perspective, which is free of time, place, or rank, we must do away with all comparative meanings.

That simple clarification rules out all meanings except *shake* and *head*. If we think of *head* as *source*, like *head-waters*, it works.

Shake also fits with the first sentence where ELOHIM is said to be hovering or shaking over the face of the waters. If you observe Dr. Tabor's note for bere'sheet, you will see the following:

> Lit "At *the* head of," Heb *Bere'sheet* in this grammatical construction is a temporal phrase meaning, "When at first . . .," see Jer 26:1 where the same form occurs. It presents the "state of things" when the creative activity begins.

Instead of a temporal statement, as is the traditional view, let's view "the state of things" as a timeless reference. Viewed in that way, it works. In any case, as bere'sheet and genesis are used, it clearly conveys the vibrating source. To shake is to vibrate. That vibration is the eternal "singing" of praise that I mentioned earlier.

If we translate *Bet* as "at" and *Roshe* as "shaking head", we get "At the shaking head," which we can view figuratively as the ever-present shaking or vibrating source of existence. If we were to substitute in these meanings, the opening of Genesis 1:1-2 would look like this: "At the shaking source of ELOHIM creating the skies and the land—and the land was desolation and emptiness; and darkness *was* over *the* face of *the* deep, and the spirit of ELOHIM was shaking over the face of the waters."

As we discussed the etymology of bere'sheet and relevant mystical experiences already, let's direct our attention to the science. According to what science has revealed, the Universe is a vibrating field of energy that traces back to the Big Bang. Energy vibrates. Light vibrates. Sound vibrates. Atoms vibrate. Even the brainwaves that we correlate to states of consciousness vibrate. The stars and planets ring with vibrations.

To get a sense of the cosmic vibrations, you might do an internet search for "Symphony of Stars: The Science of Stellar Sound Waves I NASA." There you can enjoy listening to the Universe vibrate. It's awe-inspiring.

As you can see, "At the shaking source" matches all three guides established above: the original Hebrew characters, mystical experience, and science. The ancient sages understood and science now verifies that everything is vibrating and resonating, even outer space. This vibration is the loving praise of the Witness, or put another way, the Holy Spirit. The vibration moves out from the center of the torus like a great wind blowing over grass as it vibrates into the dream of reality.

John's "Word of God" is thought by Christians to refer to Jesus of Nazareth, whom they call "Christ, the one anointed by God." While that may or may not be the case, the meaning of the Word of God is much broader and can be viewed in another way that may be more revealing and helpful to everyone, even those people who do not identify with Christianity.

The Word of God is the Spirit of God that fills the Universe with life. It is, in essence, the Consciousness within Mind, which is another way of saying the Word of God is the vibration of YHVH ELOHIM.

> "In him was life, and that life was the light of all mankind. The light shines in the darkness, and the darkness has not overcome it" (John 1:4-5).

The darkness is Mind. The Light illuminates Mind. The genesis of "objective reality" is Mind within Consciousness and Consciousness within Mind—chaos within order and order within chaos. It is Law. It is Life.

Human beings can have experiences of the Holy Spirit, and when it "comes upon you," as the Gospels often describe it, the experience can have dramatic effects on the body and mind. I described this effect in Chapter 1 as follows: "The dream was exactly the same as it had always been, but unexpectedly, at the instant where I always awoke, the moment where Jesus asks for help the second time, a surge of energy filled my body, anchoring me in the dream."

That surge of energy is the experience of the Holy Spirit. It feels like light is blowing into you. Looking up the Hebrew meaning of the "spirit of God" reveals the following: Ruach (רוּחַ) means variously "wind," "spirit," or "breath." ELOHIM can mean "great" or "god." So Ruach ELOHIM (the spirit of God) can also be interpreted as "the wind of God" or "breath of God."

You'll notice that the creative process in Genesis 2 is done through the breath of God. As a reminder, the passage is as follows: "and YHVH ELOHIM shaped the soil-creature—dust from the soil, and he blew into his two nostrils breath of life; and the soil-creature became a living life-breather."

Being filled with the Holy Spirit tends to have a number of powerful effects on the individual. One possible effect is that you feel powerfully anchored, such that if standing at the time, it might feel like your feet are welded to the ground, or the energy may move your body to do something in particular. Another common effect is to feel like you are filled with a brilliant inner light. This light provides clarity that far surpasses normal ideas of mental or emotional clarity. Finally, the experience of being filled with the Holy Spirit often proceeds powerful mystical, revelatory, or insightful experiences. Whatever the experience that accompanies being filled with the Holy Spirit, it's best not to let yourself feel special because of them. Learn from them and let them go, otherwise you will be trapped by arrogance.

Someone who has not had such experiences may assume they indicate a psychiatric disorder. Psychiatric disorders, however, are profoundly different from experiences of the Holy Spirit. The experience of the Holy Spirit produces clarity, enhanced functionality, and healthy outcomes, whereas psychiatric disorders often have the opposite effect.

Although counter-intuitive at first, it is helpful to be conscious that the Holy Spirit resides always within us, though usually we remain unconscious of it. When it is revealed, it may seem as if it came from outside you, but that is not what is actually happening. It only feels like something other than you because when it floods the body, you are completely unfamiliar with it. When the Holy Spirit is sufficiently expressing in the body, which means the sense that you are a separate identity falls away, there is a vibrant clarity, wholeness, and the realization that you have always been one with the Holy Spirit deep down.

The question you are likely to have after the Holy Spirit experience ends is how to get it back. We'll be discussing this question in the next chapter. The key takeaway from this chapter is that Pure Consciousness, Universal Mind, and the Holy Spirit are triune in their being, or three aspects of the very same thing. This triune being is you, me, the entire Universe, and beyond. There is no other.

Here is a basic practice that takes advantage of another meaning to Logos, which is "true words." Much of our inner disharmony arises simply as a result of being dishonest with ourselves and others. Practicing the logos means adjusting our words and thinking so that we are more aligned and truer in our hearts.

To be fair, it seems much easier to know when we are not being true than when we are being true, because truth can be difficult to pin down. Thus, with this exercise, notice any thoughts and language you use that does not fit with how you would think and speak if you truly loved, trusted and supported the fullness of your being.

Below is a short list of thoughts and expressions that lead us away from the fullest expression of our true nature:

Approval seeking

Assuming motivations

Attention seeking

Avoiding responsibility

Cowardly yeses

Boastfulness

Breaking your word

Casual promises

Certainty

Condemnation

Deceitfulness

Domineering

Emotional manipulation

Flattery

Gossip

Hate

Ineffectual complaint

Identifying with ideology

Minimizing responsibility

Neglectfulness

Rationalizing desires

Resentment

Self-aggrandizement

Self-deprecation (habitual)

Self-victimization

Sniveling

Snoopiness

Social positioning

Spitefulness

Tardiness (habitual)

Told you so

Unnecessary white lies

Chapter 16

You

"The coming of the kingdom of God is not something that can be observed, nor will people say, 'Here it is,' or 'There it is,' because the kingdom of God is in your midst."

— Jesus (Luke 17:20-21)

If you've sufficiently developed the "eyes to see," you will notice several hints as to the nature of the kingdom of God hidden in the above quote. The kingdom of God, also called the kingdom of Heaven, is the metaphorical paradise described as the Garden of Eden in Genesis 2.

In Hebrew, "Eden" is the name of a place or region and means "pleasure" or "bliss." The garden of Eden in Hebrew is called "Gan Eden." As Jesus was Jewish, speaking to fellow Jews, Gan Eden is what Jesus would have meant by the kingdom of God. Please consider the above quote from Luke for a moment before reading on to explore its hidden meanings.

Notice Jesus refers to the kingdom of God as coming and as being in the midst of the people simultaneously. How can it be coming and in the midst of them at the same time?

The "coming kingdom of God" is in reference to the potential of people to open up to the Eden within themselves. But that's not all that it means because the kingdom that exists within may also refer to Jesus himself, or anyone present who was a living example of a fully open heart. The hidden message is that the kingdom of God, Eden, is within *and* all around. To experience it, all that is required is to open your heart to the totality of life. But to do that, you must first open fully to yourself, and that means opening your heart fully to the serpent within you.

The serpent within the garden is not a mistake, nor is it evil. The serpent is self-consciousness, a capacity that we naked apes could not survive without. The tree of knowledge of good and bad represents knowledge, identity, logic, reason, and moral judgment. The tree of life represents the awakened state of balance where one has the capacity for identity, logic, reason, and discernment, but is no longer captured by those forces.

The kingdom of Heaven reveals itself to us when there is a balance of Universal Mind and Pure Consciousness within the human being, where instinct, detailed perception, and a grounded contextual awareness are mutually supportive. Then we are awake.

Jesus' observation that the kingdom of heaven exists within us carried three connected meanings. First, that it is coming, which indicates the potential for future realization. Second, that the kingdom of God is here, through Jesus consciously. And thirdly, the kingdom is here through each individual unconsciously. The

Garden of Eden has always been within us and will always be there. The felt experience of Eden is coming to those who are waking up to that fact through their daily life.

With our potential for harmony in life in mind, let's trace the entire process of the Witness, as it forgets its holistic nature, experiences the dream of itself as a human being, and becomes lucidly aware of its true nature within the experience of the human being.

To convey the human aspect of this story, I will have to explain through the perspective of time. Please grant that there is no other way to convey this process, for time is how humans experience life. You might bear in mind that whatever is described is actually timeless from the perspective of the Infinite.

From its open perspective, Pure Consciousness sees all possibilities and recognizes, in the face of all possible forms and expressions, that there is no other. Pure Consciousness witnesses all potentiality simultaneously. As a result of total seeing, it does not get caught up in any particular perspective.

Due to its all-inclusive awareness, it can be likened to a brilliant white light. When a human experiences the holistic perspective of Pure Consciousness they feel beauty and love beyond imagination. Words cannot come near the experience. Such individuals will probably recall the experience of Pure Consciousness as among the most (or as the most) meaningful of their lives, and many of them will begin dedicating their lives to the sharing of that perspective.

Universal Mind represents the potential of the Infinite to narrow its attention to a specific set of possibilities, to a specific identity, for example. Much like closing your eyes has the effect of blocking out the light, the experience is that of darkness. When Universal Mind narrows its attention in this way, the darkness triggers a dreamlike state that we experience as reality. Through its search, Universal Mind projects opposing ideas of itself, both positive and negative. The dual forces of order and chaos combine to create the hologram of reality, the dream of life, the dream of you.

As the Witness narrows its awareness through progressive extrapolations on projected potentials, ever more does it lose track of its unified or nondual nature. Not knowing, it naturally seeks to identify itself, much as people seek to find and maintain identity.

Essentially, Universal Mind gets lost in a dream of dual opposites that takes the energetic form of a torus. The earth emits this torus, as do all nerve centers in your body, most notably, your brain, your heart, and your gut. Each cell has a magnetic field, a torus. You are the Witness dreaming of itself as a person. You are the embodiment of the Infinite having forgotten your Infinite nature.

The Witness, having narrowed its attention, has forgotten its holistic nature. When born into the world as a human, the Witness is embodied in a state of innocence like Adam and Eve experienced in Genesis 2. This innocence remains until the human body matures through the senses and sufficiently develops the sense of self-consciousness. Self-consciousness leads to self-protective measures and a closing of the heart into a state of near constant self-absorption. You might remember this state from your teen years.

Through socialization, the child learns to control its self-absorption enough to experience generally productive relationships in society. But, regardless of their degree of success in the world, the individual feels somehow incomplete and is never fully comfortable in their own skin. This state maps onto the self-doubt and rebelliousness of Adam and Eve in Genesis 3.

At this stage of development, the human experiences a near constant low-grade inner dissatisfaction. They tend to feel not truly seen, not truly heard, yet they might actually fear being truly seen and heard. They feel distrust for themselves and others.

These feelings stem from a loss of contextual awareness that engenders a sense of separation from life. This narrow state of awareness can express itself also in a feeling of being cast out and of being unworthy of love—fundamentally, feeling alone. Consciously we may feel self-doubt, or we may feel arrogant. It's also possible that we express those things but are entirely unconscious of those expressions. Whether we express self-doubt or arrogance largely depends upon our personality type. In any case, both expressions signal deep insecurity.

The most common strategy for the individual is to seek distraction from these underlying feelings through myriad means: sleep, sex, intoxicants, entertainment, hobbies, relationships, work—anything that keeps them from feeling their inner space for too long.

Some individuals have a desire to awaken, which is to say, to see the underlying disharmony and to discover their deepest nature. This condition should not be considered morally superior, for to measure in this way would be to eat of the tree of the knowledge of good and bad.

What we can say is that for some reason, certain individuals grow tired of self-absorption, and they want to open their eyes to see themselves, others, and the world more completely. They desire to explore and understand what motivates inharmonious thoughts, feelings, and behaviors that have been negatively affecting their lives. They seek to be fully honest with themselves, authentic, and present in life. They seek to be of service, doing what is helpful, necessary, meaningful, and engaging according to their own definitions of those words.

These awakening individuals, if truly paying attention to their lives and not deferring to authorities about their inner nature, discover the meaning of repentance and atonement. They realize that being fully honest with themselves about the facets of self-absorption is repentance. Repentance means admitting where we feel shame, blame, guilt, and arrogance. Repentance means noticing and correcting the mind when it moralizes about ourselves, others, or the Universe. Through sustained awareness, those individuals stop or at least lessen the habits of labeling, condemning, cursing, and moralizing.

To complete the process, they open their hearts fully to release resentment and hatred of those negative energies within themselves and those that they project onto others. They necessarily open the heart and mind to see the actual causes of those energies by removing moralizing judgment against those energies. Removing the moralizing judgment provides true clarity. This clarity is the meaning of forgiveness. When they clearly see the causes of shame, blame, guilt, and arrogance, so long as they don't fall into shame, blame, guilt, and arrogance while seeing them, then they are clear. It helps to remember the warning from Jesus in Matthew 7:1-2, "Do not judge, or you too will be judged. For in the same way you judge others, you will be judged, and with the measure you use, it will be measured to you."

We should be mindful of the meaning of forgiveness. For many of us, the concept of forgiveness has been greatly distorted by the moralizing tendency of the mind. We humans tend to judge ourselves and others for both not forgiving and for forgiving. Forgiveness or lack thereof does not make you good or bad, superior or inferior. In fact, forgiveness is not a moral process.

Forgiveness only comes from clarity. Without clarity there can be no forgiveness. With clarity we see the stifling effect that moralizing judgment creates for all involved, and, therefore, we are far less likely to judge anyone or anything. And when we do morally judge, we are much more likely to notice and release that judgment like a hot potato. Clarity means understanding that there are reasons why people behave the way they do, even if those reasons are not known.

Forgiveness is also commonly assumed to be synonymous with the meaning of reconciliation, but forgiveness and reconciliation are not synonymous. Forgiveness means releasing others from moral judgment. Reconciliation, on the other hand, involves the decision on the part of all parties to maintain the relationship, while addressing any contentious issues.

If you have informed the other person of the unpreferred behavior, and the other person repeatedly fails to correct it, then it is reasonable and maybe healthy to omit them from your personal life. The individual with clarity realizes that who they allow into their personal life is their preference and prerogative. That is clarity.

The individual who has clarity recognizes that they can fully love someone and forgive them for poor behavior and still decide not to maintain an active relationship with them. They feel no shame, blame, guilt, arrogance, or resentment connected to maintaining or severing the relationship. They have the clarity to know what they want in their lives and what they do not want, and they acknowledge the price they pay for their actions and inactions.

The individual with clarity takes authority in their life and makes no excuses. They take care to negotiate with other people when negotiation is necessary because they recognize that avoiding necessary but uncomfortable conversations results in the buildup of resentment. They understand that resentment blocks clarity and ruins relationships.

Of course, the awakening individual understands that the light of clarity necessarily shines brightest on their own thoughts, emotions, and behaviors. The awakening individual strives to see their own motivations. With persistent observation they can see, in detail, the cause of any negative thoughts, emotions, and behaviors while maintaining a fully open heart. Seeing with a fully open heart is atonement (at-one-ment). Atonement means admitting why we think, feel, and act the way we do. Atonement is true only if the admission is without justification, minimization, shame, blame, guilt, arrogance, or resentment.

Such individuals notice that a lot of energy is wasted in useless grumbling and complaint about things that they have no control over. And with that sustained awareness, ineffectual complaint fades from their lives. This one change saves them a great deal of time and energy that they can then direct toward what they feel is necessary, helpful, meaningful, and engaging. They feel greatly empowered by this simple change.

With sustained daily application of *the principle*, a sense of expansiveness or spaciousness grows within the awakening individual. With persistence, it extends beyond the flesh and encompasses the environment around them. Such individuals start to feel as though this spaciousness is the common denominator of awareness behind everyone's hearts and minds, even though most people are entirely unconscious of this shared denominator.

The highly awakened individual can feel this spaciousness in themselves, in animals, in trees, in rocks, in everything. And as that feeling grows stronger, ever less do they believe that they are their personality, thoughts, emotions, or their life story. They may still get caught up in their identity, thoughts, emotions, and story from time to time, but they come out of the spell relatively quickly. As they develop this ability to disidentify with those energies, those forces lose sway over their lives. Such individuals are, in a sense, free in a way that other people are not.

Through open-hearted spacious awareness that should not be equated to personality traits such as agreeableness or openness to experience, those who live with it consciously can see that other people are trapped in their minds, feeling alone, separate, and unworthy of love, just as they once felt. They can see the shame, blame, guilt, and arrogance unconsciously motivate the lives of just about everyone. And they know that those forces result in many of the decisions that people believe they are freely choosing.

They can also see that people are trapped and looking for distraction or escape routes. But the awakening individual knows that there is no escaping reality. The awakening individual sees clearly that the desire to measure their fundamental nature, which is to moralize the self, only adds to our deep insecurity and sense of aloneness. Temporarily closing awareness to those uncomfortable feelings combined with being personally identified with them further fuels the state of insecurity. The person living in clarity sees that the way out of this nightmare is to open awareness to these feelings, to face fears, to admit the myriad ways in which they might have been shaming, blaming, guilting, and stroking themselves and others.

Thus, the awakening process can lead us toward a deeply embodied honesty. Often, we can recognize that the lofty values that we may have striven for, like world peace, helping others, empathy, kindness, and love, in many cases may have been motivated by energies far less noble, such as comfort, approval seeking, or seeing oneself as morally upright or spiritual.

Many people may have worked tremendously hard at achieving moral goals, but as they awaken and begin to see behind the curtain of their minds, they are likely to notice some degree of image consciousness with regard to these goals, which is to say they could have been seeking approval or validation of their worthiness. The combined practice of being deeply honest with themselves and opening the heart leads people seeking to live in clarity through a very healthy form of discomfort that ultimately reveals the kingdom of Heaven within. Their daily practice is a sustained love for *all-that-is*. This love changes the motivations behind their aims and how they do just about everything.

They realize that the kingdom of Heaven, when experienced through a human body, should not be equated with comfort. In reality, the experience is a vibrant aliveness, akin to what athletes often describe as being "in the zone." Imagine riding the lightning when you are the lightning. Being in Eden means you are fully YOU.

So, as you can see, through the awakening process, you start out expansively like Genesis 1, narrow through the manifestation of an innocent body, as with Genesis 2, become self-absorbed through self-consciousness, like what happens in Genesis 3, and finally, through self-awareness, you expand yet again, while still alive, which is the return to Eden. The shape is like that of an hourglass or the mathematical figure for infinity.

You have now reached the most essential question about your experience with this book. How do you know if *the principle* of *no other* is practical and transformative?

The only way to know is to prove it through your own life. You can do this by committing to maintaining a fully open, positive heart as we saw in the creation story of Genesis 1. You can begin serving all of life innocently as Genesis 2 reminds us to do. And you can start noticing and reducing deceitful, unhelpful thoughts and expressions such as moralizing, labeling, and complaining about yourself, others, and the Universe to avoid the trap of self-absorption modeled in Genesis 3.

With loving persistence, with commitment and long-term follow-through in daily life, you will know for yourself that you are the Infinite, as is everyone and everything. If you do this, what I can say with near certainty is that it's going to challenge you to the depth of your being.

Are you ready for the most inspiring journey a person can undertake? Are you ready to be fully YOU?

With you on the path,

Richard L. Haight
Oct 10, 2021

P.S. If you enjoyed this book, please consider leaving a review where you purchased *The Genesis Code*.

P.P.S. If you would like to discuss *The Genesis Code* with other readers, you can join The Genesis Code Readers' Group here: https://www.facebook.com/groups/thegenesiscode

THE BOOK OF GENESIS

A NEW TRANSLATION FROM THE

TRANSPARENT ENGLISH BIBLE

JAMES D. TABOR

GENESIS 2000 PRESS

Amazon link for print or Kindle:

https://www.amazon.com/dp/B08GGB8X84

The Tabor Translation Reader's Guide

Italic Type indicates words **not** in the Hebrew but supplied for smoother English style

Names or terms for God such as ELOHIM, YHVH, or ADONAI are indicated in all CAPS

Chapter 3:14 And YHVH ELOHIM said to the Nachash, "Because you have done this, cursed *are* you above every animal, and above every living thing of the field; upon your belly you will walk, and dust you will eat, all the days of your life². 15 And hatred I will place between you and between the woman, and between your seed and between her seed;¹ *he* will strike² you—*on the* head, and *you* will strike him—*on the* heel." 16 To the woman he said, "Causing to be many—I will *surely* cause to be many!—your distress³ and your pregnancy; in distress you will bring forth sons, and toward your man⁴ *will be* your craving, and *he* will rule with⁵ you." 17 And to Adam⁶ he said, "Because you hearkened to⁷ the voice of your woman, and you ate from the tree that I charged you saying, 'You shall not eat from it,' cursed *is* the soil on account of you. In distress⁸ you will eat *of* it all the days of your life²; 18 and thorn and thistle it will sprout for you, and you will eat the plant of the field. 19 In the sweat of your two nostrils you will eat bread, until you return to the soil, for from it you were taken; for dust you *are*, and to dust you will return."

Explanatory footnotes are at the bottom of the page and indicated by a superscript number²

Words in **bold italics** indicate special emphasis in the Hebrew

These special "white spaces" are in the original Hebrew manuscripts, indicating a break in thought or an emphasis of a section of text

Masculine™ Feminine^f Singular^s Plural^p Causitive^c and the Definite^d article are indicated by these tiny superscript letters

---

¹ Or "offspring," Heb *zera'* normally refers to male "seed," but can refer to female reproduction (Gen 16:10; Lev 12:2).
² Or "bruise."
³ Or "sorrow," same word as v. 17b.
⁴ Heb *'ish*.
⁵ I.e., with regard to.
⁶ Heb *'adam*, *soul*-man, without the article, probably here the proper name.
⁷ Lit "heard to."
⁸ Or "sorrow," same word as v. 16.

The Transparent English Version of the Book of Genesis

(Bere'sheet)[1]

Chapter **1:1** At *the* first[f2] of ELOHIM[3] creating the skies and the land—**2** and the land was[4] desolation and emptiness; and darkness *was* over *the* face[p] of *the* deep, and the spirit[5] of ELOHIM was hovering[6] over the face[p] of the waters—**3** and ELOHIM said, "Let there be light"; and it was light. **4** And ELOHIM saw the light, that *it was* good; and ELOHIM separated between the light and between the darkness.[7] **5** And ELOHIM called to the light "day,"[8]

---

1 The books of the Hebrew Bible are named from their opening words: here *Bere'sheet*, meaning "At *the* first of . . . "

2 Lit "At *the* head of," Heb *Bere'sheet* in this grammatical construction is a temporal phrase meaning, "When at first . . .," see Jer 26:1 where the same form occurs. It presents the "state of things" when the creative activity begins.

3 ELOHIM is a plural noun, but often functions as a collective singular, taking a singular verb. It is related to the Hebrew terms: *'eloah* and *'el*, meaning God, god, power, or mighty one, and can refer to judges and leaders, heavenly beings, the gods of the nations, or the one God of Israel.

4 Or "became."

5 Heb *ruach*, lit "wind," see Gen 7:1.

6 I.e., "fluttering," or "shaking," see Deut 32:11; Jer 23:9, the only two other places this verb is used, always in an intensive form (Piel).

7 I.e., separated the light from the darkness.

8 DSS "daytime."

and to the darkness he called "night." And it was evening and it was morning—day one.[9]

6 And ELOHIM said, "Let there be an expanse in the middle of the waters, and let there be a separating between waters to waters." **7** And ELOHIM made[10] the expanse, and he separated between the waters that *were* from under the expanse, and between the waters that *were* from upon the expanse. And it was thus. **8** And ELOHIM called to the expanse "skies." And it was evening and it was morning, a second day.

9 And ELOHIM said, "Let the waters under the skies be gathered toward one place,[11] and let the dry *land* be seen." And it was thus. **10** And ELOHIM called to the dry *land* "land," and to the collection of the waters he called "seas." And ELOHIM saw that *it was* good. **11** And ELOHIM said, "Let the land sprout[c] *the* sprout, a plant seeding seed, a fruit tree making[12] fruit, according to its type, its seed, within it, upon the land." And it was thus. **12** And the land made *the* sprout go out[c], a plant seeding seed according to its type, and a tree making[13] fruit, its seed, within it, according to its type. And ELOHIM saw that *it was* good. **13** And it was evening and it was morning, a third day.

14 And ELOHIM said, "Let there be lights in the expanse of the skies, to separate between the day and between the night; and they

---

9 These paragraph breaks, as well as the smaller "white space" divisions (see Gen 3:16-17), are taken from the Hebrew text and are reproduced precisely throughout this translation, as explained in the Introduction.
10 Or "did."
11 DSS "one gathering," producing alliteration with the verb "gathered."
12 Or "doing."
13 Or "doing."

will be[14] for signs, and for appointed times,[15] and for days and years,[16] **15** and they will be for lights in the expanse of the skies, to make light[c] upon the land." And it was thus. **16** And ELOHIM made[17] the two large lights—the large light for rule of the day, and the small light for rule of the night—and the stars. **17** And ELOHIM gave them in the expanse of the skies, to make light[c] upon the land, **18** and to rule in the day and in the night, and to separate between the light and between the darkness. And ELOHIM saw that *it was* good. **19** And it was evening and it was morning, a fourth day.

20 And ELOHIM said, "Let the waters swarm a swarm of living life-breathers[s],[18] and let *the* flyer fly upon the land, upon the face[p] of the expanse of the skies." **21** And ELOHIM created the large *water*-beasts,[19] and every living[d] life-breather that moves about, *with* which the waters swarm, according to their type, and every winged flyer, according to its type. And ELOHIM saw that *it was* good. **22** And ELOHIM blessed them saying, "Bear fruit and be abundant and fill the waters in the seas, and let the flyer[20] be abundant in the land." **23** And it was evening and it was morning, a fifth day.

24 And ELOHIM said, "Let the land make a living life-breather go out[c] according to its type: animal, and moving thing, and living

---

14 DSS "and they were"; this reading seems to support the possibility of the direct quotation ending after ". . . between the night," as some translators have suggested.

15 Heb *mo'adim*, "appointed times," whether astronomical, divine, or human.

16 DSS "for years."

17 Or "did."

18 Heb *nephesh chayyah*, refers to breathing life of all types; the same term is used in 1:24 for land animals and in 2:7 for humans.

19 Heb *tanin*, refers to any fierce monster-like creature, usually in the sea or rivers. See Gen 1:21; Exo 7:9; Psa 91:13; Isa 27:1; Ezk 29:3

20 DSS "the flying thing will be abundant."

thing of land according to its type." And it was thus. **25** And ELOHIM made[21] the living thing of the land, according to its type, and the animal according to its type, and every moving thing of the soil according to its type. And ELOHIM saw that *it was* good. **26** And ELOHIM said, "Let us make[22] soil-creature[23] in our image, according to our likeness, and let them govern in[24] the fish of the sea, and with the flyer of the skies, and in the animals[s], and in all the land,[25] and in every moving thing that moves about upon the land." **27** And ELOHIM created the soil-creature in his image: in the image of ELOHIM he created him, a male and a female he created them. **28** And ELOHIM blessed them and ELOHIM said to them, "Bear fruit and be abundant and fill the land; and subdue, and govern in the fish of the sea, and in the flyer of the skies, and in every living thing that moves about upon the land." **29** And ELOHIM said, "Look!—I have given to you[p] every plant seeding seed that *is* upon the face[p] of all the land, and every tree[d], in which *there is* fruit of a tree, seeding seed; to you[p] it will be for an eatable *thing*. **30** And to every living thing of the land, and to every flyer of the skies, and to every moving about thing on the land, that in it *is* living life-breath[26]—every green plant *is* for an eatable *thing*." And it was thus. **31** And ELOHIM saw all that he had made,[27] and look!—*it was* exceedingly good. And it was evening and it was morning, the sixth day.

---

21 Or "did."

22 Or "do."

23 Heb *'adam*, from *'adamah*, "soil," or "red soil."

24 I.e., in regard to, here and v. 28.

25 Syriac "over all the animals of the land."

26 Heb *nephesh chayyah*, used of humans in Gen 2:7.

27 Or "done."

Chapter **2:1** And the skies and the land and all their company[28] were finished. **2** And ELOHIM finished on the seventh day his work that he did, and he ceased[29] on the seventh day[30] from all his work that he did. **3** And ELOHIM blessed the seventh day, and he set it apart, because on it he ceased from all his work that ELOHIM created to do.

4 These *are* **the bringings-forth of the skies and the land**[31] in their being created. In *the* day of the making[32] of YHVH[33] ELOHIM, land and skies, **5** and no shrub of the field was before *that* on the land, and no plant of the field had before *that* sprouted—for YHVH ELOHIM had not made rain[c] on the land, and there *was* no soil-creature to service the soil; **6** and a flow[34] would go up from the land, and it made drink[c] all the face[p] of the soil—**7** and YHVH ELOHIM shaped the soil-creature—dust from the soil,[35] and he blew into his two nostrils breath[36] of life[p]; and the soil-creature became a living life-breather.[37] **8** And YHVH ELOHIM planted a garden in Eden,[38] at the east; and there he placed the soil-creature whom he shaped. **9** And YHVH ELOHIM made sprout[c] from the

---

28 Or "army," Heb *tzava'*, refers to a gathering or mustering.

29 Heb *shavat*, or "rested," in the sense of halting.

30 LXX, Syriac, and SP read "sixth day" here.

31 Genesis has ten divisions, each beginning with the phrase "These *are* the bringings-forth of . . ." and these are indicated in this translation by **bold type**.

32 Lit "doing."

33 Name of the God of Israel יהוה (Tetragrammaton), traditionally Yahveh, or Yehovah; translated LORD in most English versions but here left as four letters without vowels.

34 Or "mist," meaning uncertain, used only here and Job 36:27.

35 Heb *'adamah*, from which the term *"soil-creature"* (*'adam*) is derived.

36 Heb *nishamah*, cf. Gen 7:15,22 where a different term is used.

37 Heb *nephesh chayyah*, same term as in 1:20,21,24, refers to breathing life of all type, whether animal or human. The standard English translation of "soul" is accordingly misleading.

38 Name of a place or region, meaning "pleasure" or "bliss."

soil every tree desired for sight and good for an eatable *thing*; and the tree of life[p] in the middle of the garden, and the tree of the knowledge of good and bad. **10** And a river goes out from Eden to make drink[c] the garden, and from there it is separated and it becomes four heads. **11** The name of the one *is* Pishon;[39] it goes around all the land of the Havilah, where there *is* gold[d], **12** and the gold of that land *is* good; there *are* bdellium and the onyx stone. **13** And the name of the second river *is* Gihon;[40] it goes around all the land of Cush.[41] **14** And the name of the third river *is* Hiddekel;[42] it *is* the one walking east of Assyria. And the fourth river—it *is* Euphrates.[43] **15** And YHVH ELOHIM took the soil-creature and made him rest[c] in the garden of Eden, to service it and to guard it. **16** And YHVH ELOHIM *laid* charge upon the soil-creature, saying, "From every tree of the garden, eating—you will *surely* eat![44] **17** And from the tree of the knowledge of good and bad, you will not eat from it; for on *the* day you eat from it, dying—you will *surely* die!"[45] **18** And YHVH ELOHIM said, "Not good—the soil-creature being by himself, I will make[46] for him a help, as his *one* before."[47] **19** And YHVH ELOHIM shaped from the soil every living thing of the field, and every flyer of the skies, and he made come[c] toward the soil-creature to see what he would call to it; and whatever the soil-creature would call to it—*each* living life-breather—that *was* its name. **20** And the soil-creature called names

---

39 Possibly from verb *push*, "to leap," "spread about."
40 Meaning, "to gush forth."
41 Uncertain, perhaps the lands of the southern Nile.
42 Meaning uncertain; LXX reads Tigris.
43 Heb *Pherat*, "fruitfulness."
44 Double use of the verb indicates emphasis.
45 Double use of the verb indicates emphasis.
46 Or "do."
47 I.e., one facing him, before or opposite him, as his corresponding counterpart.

to every animal, and to the flyer of the skies, and to every living thing of the field; and to *Soil-creature*[48] he did not find a help, as his *one* before.[49] **21** And YHVH ELOHIM made a deep sleep fall[c] upon the soil-creature, and he slept; and he took one from his sides, and he closed flesh under it. **22** And YHVH ELOHIM built the side that he took from the soil-creature into a woman, and he made her come[c] toward the soil-creature. **23** And the soil-creature said, "This one this time—bone of my bones, and flesh of my flesh! To this one will be called "woman,"[50] because from a man[51] this one was taken." **24** Therefore a man[52] will leave his father and his mother, and join[53] with his woman, and they become one flesh. **25** And the *two* of them were nude,[54]—the soil-creature and his woman—and they were not ashamed. chapter **3:1** And the Nachash[55] was shrewd[56]—from[57] every living thing of the field that YHVH ELOHIM made.[58] And he said toward the woman, "Did ELOHIM indeed say, 'You[p] may not eat from any tree of the garden'?" **2** And the woman said toward the Nachash, "From the fruit of the trees[s] of the garden we may eat; **3** and from the fruit of the tree that is in the middle of the garden, ELOHIM said, 'You[p] will not eat from it,

---

48 Heb *'adam*, "*soil-creature*," without the article, that some have taken as the proper name, "Adam."

49 See note on v. 18.

50 Heb *'ishah*.

51 Heb *'ish*.

52 Heb *'ish*.

53 I.e., to stick to, as in soldering.

54 Heb *'arumim*, word play with "shrewd" in the following verse.

55 Heb *nachash*, usually a snake, but it can also refer to a sea creature (Amos 9:3; Isa 27:1), the root meaning "shine" (like brass) or "hiss" as in enchantment.

56 Heb *'arum*, see previous verse; "nude" comes from the same root, meaning "smooth" or "slick."

57 I.e., more shrewd in contrast with ("away from") any other.

58 Or "did."

and you will not touch it, lest you die.'" **4** And the Nachash said toward the woman, "Dying—you[P] will not *surely* die![59] **5** For ELOHIM knows that in *the* day you[P] eat from it that your eyes will be opened and you[P] will be as ELOHIM knowing[P] good and bad." **6** And the woman saw that the tree *was* good for an eatable *thing*, and that it *was* a longing to the eyes, and the tree *was* desirable for causing insight[c], and she took from its fruit and she ate; and she gave also to her man[60] with her, and he ate. **7** And the eyes of the two of them were opened, and they knew that they *were* nude; and they sewed leaves[s] of a fig tree and they made[61] for themselves loin-cloths. **8** And they heard the voice[62] of YHVH ELOHIM walking about[63] in the garden in the wind[64] of the day, and the soil-creature made himself hidden[c]—and his woman—from the face[P] of YHVH ELOHIM in the middle of the trees[s] of the garden. **9** And YHVH ELOHIM called toward the *soil-creature*, and he said to him, "Where *are* you?" **10** And he said, "Your voice[65] I heard in the garden, and I feared, for I *was* nude; and I was hidden." **11** And he said, "Who told to you that you *were* nude? From the tree that I charged you 'so as not to eat from it,' have you eaten?" **12** And the soil-creature said, "The woman, that—you gave her *to be* with me—*she* gave to me from the tree, and I ate." **13** And YHVH ELOHIM said to the woman, "What *is* this you have done?" And the woman said, "The Nachash, he deceived me, and I ate." **14** And YHVH ELOHIM said toward the Nachash, "Because you have

---

59 Double use of the verb indicates emphasis.
60 Heb *'ish*.
61 Or "did for themselves."
62 I.e., sound; in Hebrew "voice" is used as a metaphor for all kinds of sounds.
63 This form of the verb carries an iterative meaning, thus "to walk back and forth."
64 I.e., breeze.
65 I.e., sound, in Hebrew "voice" is used as a metaphor for all kinds of sounds.

done this, cursed *are* you above every animal, and above every living thing of the field; upon your belly you will walk, and dust you will eat, all the days of your life[p]. **15** And hostility I will set between you and between the woman, and between your seed and between her seed;[66] *he* will strike[67] you—*on the* head, and *you* will strike him—*on the* heel." **16** Toward the woman he said, "Making abundant[c]—I will *surely* make abundant[c]![68]—your distress[69] and your pregnancy; in distress you will bring forth sons, and toward your man[70] *will be* your craving, and *he* will rule in you."[71] **17** And to *Soil-creature*[72] he said, "Because you hearkened to[73] the voice of your woman, and you ate from the tree that I charged you saying, 'You will not eat from it,' cursed *is* the soil on account of you. In distress[74] you will eat it all the days of your life[p]; **18** and thorn and thistle it will sprout for you, and you will eat the plant of the field. **19** In the sweat of your two nostrils you will eat bread, until you return toward the soil, for from it you were taken; for dust you *are*, and toward dust you will return." **20** And the soil-creature called the name of his woman Eve,[75] for *she* was mother of all living. **21** And YHVH ELOHIM made[76] for *Soil-creature*[77] and his woman, robes of skin, and he dressed them.

---

66 Or "offspring," Heb *zera'* normally refers to male "seed," but can refer to female reproduction as well (Gen 16:10; Lev 12:2).

67 Or "bruise."

68 Double use of the verb indicates emphasis.

69 Or "sorrow," same word as v. 17b.

70 Heb *'ish.*

71 I.e., with regard to; cf. Gen 4:7, same expression used.

72 Heb *'adam,* "soil-creature," without the article, probably the proper name, "Adam."

73 Lit "heard to."

74 Or "sorrow," "hardship," same word as v. 16.

75 Heb *chavah,* meaning "living."

76 Or "did."

77 Heb *'adam,* "soil-creature," without the article, probably the proper name, "Adam."

22 And YHVH ELOHIM said, "Look!—the soil-creature has become like one from us,[78] to know good and bad; and now, lest he send forth his hand and take also from the tree of life[p], and eat, and live for an age . . . !"[79]—**23** And YHVH ELOHIM sent[80] him from the garden of Eden, to service the soil from which he was taken. **24** And he drove out[81] the soil-creature, and he made dwell[c] at the east of the garden of Eden, the cherubim, and the flame of the sword that was revolving, to guard the way of the tree of life[p].

The Book of Genesis Amazon link for print or Kindle:
https://www.amazon.com/dp/B08GGB8X84

---

78 Or "from him," pronoun can mean "us" or "him" here.
79 I.e., continually; Heb idiom referring to an undetermined time into the future or in the past. The sentence is incomplete and breaks off without finishing the thought.
80 Intensive form of the verb (Piel)
81 Intensive form of the verb (Piel).

Appendix

Helpful Practices

Chapter 9 — Practicing Praise

Please take a moment to visualize the target of each praise and then read aloud the praise while feeling the vibrations of the words as they are uttered toward the intended target.

For the best effect, leave off intellectualizing for now; just visualize and feel the body as you speak the words with intention. The words without the visualization and feeling will never get us there.

1. Light — "And God sees the light, that *it is* God"
2. Land and seas — "And God sees that *it is* God"
3. Plants and trees — "And God sees that *it is* God"
4. Sun, moon, stars — "And God sees that *it is* God"
5. Water creatures and flyers — "And God sees that *it is* God"
6. Land creatures— "And God sees that *it is* God"
7. All that is — "And God sees all that is, and look!—*it is* exceedingly God."

Look in the mirror, and while feeling your entire body, repeat and feel, "And God sees that I am God."

Practice and a little light stretching to release tension will help resolve the unhelpful judgment and feelings of separation held within the subconscious mind.

Now, look around you. To everyone and everything you see, repeat with feeling, "And God sees that it is completely, seamlessly God."

Chapter 10 — Caretaking

Think about your life. Is there anything that you do or did that feels like true caretaking? It would be an act of service, done lovingly, that gains you nothing at the level of ego. What we are indicating is a communion where everyone is served, including you, without a sense of self-absorption or codependency regarding the service. Whatever it is that you do that fits this definition is an activity that is in alignment with your truest nature, the Infinite within you. Whatever that activity is benefits everyone and everything in some way. You might allow yourself to do more of that.

Artistic, creative, and inspiring activities are best included in the caretaking category, for they nourish the soul. They are caretaking, so long as you partake in them innocently, joyfully, with all of your being, and share them with an open heart, unconcerned about how you might be judged. Becoming well-known or accepting money for the products of these nourishing activities is fine so long as reputation and wealth are not the primary motivating forces.

Chapter 11 — Reducing the Habit of Moral Judgment

Spend some time each day taking an account of the moments during the day when you measured or judged your fundamental value or that of another person. Notice when you felt shame, blame, guilt, or arrogance. Let go those feelings, for they are not helpful.

Instead of self-flagellating with ineffectual energies like moral judgment and perpetuating the suffering of Adam and Eve, simply consider what you would prefer in your life if you truly loved yourself and wanted to be the fullest you possible. Do you prefer to continue the behavior that you are judging yourself and others for? If not, do less of it, and do a bit more of what takes you in a healthy direction.

By reducing moral judgment, doing less of what is unhealthy for your long-term good, and doing more of what is healthy, your example supports others to make healthy changes as well as to be free of moral judgment. With daily persistence, this practice can bring about tremendous inner clarity and liberation. And remember, there is not, nor was there ever, an original sin.

Chapter 13 — Vibrant Silence Exercise

Practicing vibrant silence in your daily life can reveal a sense of the ever-present moment that can be tremendously transformational in your life. The key is pausing to experience the vibrant presence of the moment and noticing what prevents you from fully entering that experience. If you work to correct the blockages while practicing vibrant silence, over time, the experience becomes more accessible. Eventually your life becomes the conscious embodiment of vibrant presence.

Chapter 13 — Unifying Light Exercise

Spend a few minutes per day practicing this simple visualization exercise. Make yourself comfortable and close your eyes. Imagine that beneath or behind your perception of the world a brilliant white light unifies everyone and everything in unconditional love.

Don't overthink this exercise. Make no effort to analyze or turn this practice into a philosophy or ideology. Instead, allow yourself to be innocent like a young child during this exercise. Imagine the entire Universe aglow with a warm, embracing love. Imagine your body also suffused with this light. Release all judgment against yourself, your body, others (including your enemies), and the Universe. Be with love to the extent that you can for just a few minutes each day.

With practice you will be able to do this with your eyes open, but for many people, it is easier to begin with closed eyes. You might try it both ways each day to train the brain to be flexible with this exercise.

Chapter 14 — Breaking Free of Labels

A healthy exercise that you might actively apply throughout your day is to notice whenever you label yourself as being this or that. The most obvious such labels to notice are when you label yourself as being "good" or "bad." But any label that you really identify with, such as your job title, your social or economic position, your worthiness, et cetera, all deserve attention. Just as importantly, you might note resistance to any labels that you strongly identify against, such as "I'm not a liar" or "I'm not stingy." Maintaining such labels can be very limiting and prevent healthy life improvement.

You might also take note of when you lock others into labels. It's so easy to do. When we believe others are the labels that we have psychically attached to them, it becomes very difficult for those people to break free without severing the relationship. Set them free by disbelieving the labels. In your heart, you might discount even the labels that they apply to themselves.

The aim of this exercise is to touch base with your essential, undefined nature little by little throughout your day. When you notice a label arise in your mind, take note of it and remind yourself that in essence you are *no thing* in particular. Allow yourself a moment to feel what it is to be without any thought. Even a few seconds here and there helps.

Chapter 15 — True Words Practice

This is a basic practice that takes advantage of another meaning to Logos, which is "true words." Much of our inner disharmony arises simply as a result of being dishonest with ourselves and others. Practicing the logos means adjusting our words and thinking so that we are more aligned and truer in our hearts.

To be fair, it seems much easier to know when we are not being true than when we are being true, because truth can be difficult to pin down. Thus, with this exercise, notice any thoughts and language you use that doesn't fit with how you would think and speak if you truly loved, trusted and supported the fullness of your being.

Here is a short list of thoughts and expressions that lead us away from the fullest expression of our true nature:

Approval seeking	Ineffectual complaint
Assuming motivations	Identifying with ideology
Attention seeking	Minimizing responsibility
Avoiding responsibility	Neglectfulness
Cowardly yeses	Rationalizing desires

Boastfulness	Resentment
Breaking your word	Self-aggrandizement
Casual promises	Self-deprecation (habitual)
Certainty	Self-victimization
Condemnation	Sniveling
Deceitfulness	Snoopiness
Domineering	Social positioning
Emotional manipulation	Spitefulness
Flattery	Tardiness (habitual)
Gossip	Told you so
Hate	Unnecessary white lies
Idealizing	Willful ignorance

Glossary of Terms

Eden Synonymous with the kingdom of Heaven; paradise

Elohim The plural of El, which means deity. Elohim is considered the creator of the universe, as reflected in Genesis 1. See Universal Mind.

Pure Consciousness The unchanging foundation of perception at the core of all-that-is. Relates to YHVH in this work.

Logos Greek for "true words;" also synonymous with The Holy Spirit in Christianity.

Self-absorption Being completely caught up in your own perspective, image, and life story.

Self-consciousness Anticipating and assuming you know how others view you.

The Code The map of Genesis that indicates the principle and the path that humans must take to return to harmony.

The Holy Spirit The vibration of the Universe.

The Infinite A general term that encompasses all aspects of what might be called God.

The kingdom of Heaven Synonymous with the garden of Eden; paradise.

The principle The guiding principle of pure consciousness; there is *no other*.

The satan   The obstacle, judge, prosecutor, deceiver.

The Serpent   The spirit of self-absorption within each of us.

The tree of life   Spatial awareness, feeling, trust, empathy, big picture point of view.

The tree of the knowledge of good and bad   Self-consciousness, desire for certainty knowledge, myopic perspective, self-identity, moral judgment.

The Witness   A general term that encompasses all aspects of what might be called God.

The Word of God   Synonymous with The Holy Spirit.

Tetragrammaton   The four-letter Hebrew word יהוה, usually transliterated YHWH, YHVH, or JHVH, indicating the God of Israel.

Torus   A geometric shape like that of a ring or a donut with a hole.

Tori   Plural for torus.

Universal Mind   The aspect of the Witness that generates the hologram-like experience of the Universe. Relates to Elohim in this work.

YHVH   The tetragrammaton, the four-letter Hebrew word יהוה, usually indicating the God of Israel.

Acknowledgments

First, I would like to share my heartfelt appreciation to Barbara Becker and Linda LaTores for their assistance with research throughout this project.

I would also like to thank Mark Lyon, Irene Critchley, and Kathleen Kellaigh, along with Barbara Becker and Linda LaTores for the time and effort they invested to help improve the text. Their suggestions, questions, and their eye for grammatical faux pas greatly improved this book.

I thank Ted Noble, Jenn Coelho, Lisa Williams, Phillip Garver, and Chris Robertson for their feedback on the final draft of the manuscript.

I offer my deepest gratitude to my copy-editor Hester Lee Furey for the exacting excellence that she pours into her work. Working with Lee has been an education and an honor. And to Oriana Gatta, whose proofreading and content suggestions took the book to the next level, I share great gratitude.

I share my deep appreciation of Professor James D. Tabor for his generous support. I reached out to Dr. Tabor seeking permission to use the entirety of Chapters 1-3 of his new Transparent English Bible translation of *The Book of Genesis*, which he promptly gave. Dr. Tabor exceeded my hopes, even sending the original manuscript files so that I could copy and paste the content in its entirety, so as to keep everything in context. James D. Tabor's translation is stunning. If you are looking for a translation that catches the essence of the original Hebrew, look no further.

I offer up my appreciation to The Brothers Reed for supporting this book with their beautifully deep and soulfully touching song, "Irish Hymn". The Brother's Reed is a local band with real heart, creativity, and talent. I wish them the best with their music and their loves.

Finally, I thank those ancient unnamed individuals who, from generation to generation, strove to earnestly pass on the stories that we know of as the Book of Genesis. Were it not for their efforts, there would be no record of the path to inner freedom that they carefully protected.

The Warrior's Meditation Preview

2020 Gold Winner of the Readers' Favorite Awards, *The Warrior's Meditation* teaches the original, instinctive, non-religious form of meditation that has been all but lost to the world. Richard L. Haight, instructor of four Samurai arts, shares the best-kept secret in self-improvement, cognitive development, and stress-relief in the world.

You may wonder how the Samurai's experience bears any resemblance to your modern life. Just like the Samurai, we need a meditation that allows our actions in a high-pressure, fast-paced world to flow from a depth of awareness. The Warrior's Meditation helps you naturally access and express from that depth.

The Warrior's Meditation is flexible in application, which allows it to blend with whatever your day has in store. Through short daily sessions, the many scientifically verified cognitive and physical health benefits of daily meditation will open up to you. No longer do you need to retreat from life to meditate, for with *The Warrior's Meditation*, you can bring calm, clear awareness and vibrant life with you wherever you are. Eventually, you will fully embody meditation as a way of being, not just of doing.

Unshakable Awareness Preview

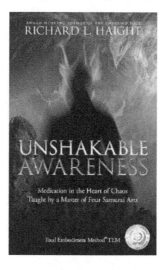

2021 Gold Winner of the Readers' Favorite Awards, *Unshakable Awareness* teaches how to stay present, clear-minded and calm when facing unpredictable life events. It offers a recipe for grounded presence when life is challenging.

Through *Unshakable Awareness* you will access meditative awareness in imperfect conditions—with your eyes open, during your active daily life. Once you get the hang of it, your ability to tap into and sustain deep meditative clarity through activities and pressures of all sorts will vastly improve, as will the quality of your life. Regardless of your background or experience level, if you tackle the challenges with a positive attitude, you will be utterly amazed at your rapid progress.

Throughout your training, you will make use of a powerful progress assessment system born of ancient lost wisdom. You will get clear, daily feedback on your improvement, which will inspire you to take on even greater challenges and realize yet further awareness possibilities and health benefits. Included are a downloadable step-by-step workbook and training schedule to help keep you on track.

The Unbound Soul Preview

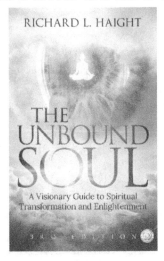

RICHARD L. HAIGHT

THE UNBOUND SOUL

A Visionary Guide to Spiritual Transformation and Enlightenment

3RD EDITION

"One of the best Consciousness books of all time"
—BookAuthority

2019 Gold Winner of the Readers' Favorite Awards and bestseller in multiple spirituality, meditation, and self-help categories, *The Unbound Soul* is a fresh, highly acclaimed spiritual guide that tells of one man's struggle to free his soul while guiding the reader to their own inner freedom.

The Unbound Soul is a memoir that tells the true story of a young boy, who in the midst of a vision, dedicates his life to spiritual awakening. As he matures, this promise leads him across the globe, gathering ancient knowledge and mastering martial, healing, and meditation arts.

But *The Unbound Soul* is so much more than a memoir. It is a powerful guide that reveals the profoundly simple yet elusive truth that illuminates your life and provides a set of powerful awareness tools to assist you on your personal path. *The Unbound Soul* is really about you and your path toward practical realization in everyday life.

About the Author

Richard L. Haight is the three-time award-winning author of *The Warrior's Meditation, Unshakable Awareness,* and *The Unbound Soul,* and he is an advanced instructor of martial, meditation and healing arts. Richard began formal martial arts training at age 12 and moved to Japan at the age of 24 to advance his training with masters of the sword, staff, and aiki-jujutsu.

Haight lived and trained in Japan for 15 years while teaching middle-school English as a foreign language. There he married his wife Teruko, and received instructional licenses in four Samurai arts and one therapy art called Sotai-ho.

Through his flexible, highly practical teachings, Richard Haight is helping to ignite a worldwide movement for personal transformation that is free of all constraints and open to anyone of any level. Richard Haight now lives and teaches in southern Oregon, U.S.A.

Contact

Here are some ways to connect with Richard Haight's teachings:

- Email: contact@richardlhaight.com
- Website: https://richardlhaight.com
- One-Month Trial Meditation Class
  https://richardlhaight.com/services
- Publishing Notifications:
  https://richardlhaight.com/notifications
- YouTube: Tools of Spiritual Awakening with Richard L Haight
- Facebook: https://facebook.com/richardlhaightauthor
- The Genesis Code Readers' Group:
  https://www.facebook.com/groups/thegenesiscode

Daily Guided Meditation
Training with Richard Haight

There are many practices included in The Genesis Code to aid in the process of consciously reentering the metaphorical Eden. Daily application is the key. As a part of my own path, I share a form of meditation that aids in the embodiment of *the principle*. I call this practice Total Embodiment Meditation (TEM). We practice for 15 minutes each day, and it makes a huge difference.

If you would like join me in the practice of this meditation, you can get a 30-day trial of my TEM daily guided meditation. Thousands of people are doing it every day. I hope to see you there!

Visit: https://richardlhaight.com/services

Made in the USA
Coppell, TX
20 June 2023

18324976R00105